PRAISE FOR *1-2-3*
IN THE CLASSROOM

What teachers are saying:

"**If you only have time to read one book** about managing student behavior, **make it this one.**"

"**Do you feel like you're at your wits' end** with your uncontrollable classroom? If the answer is yes, then **this book is definitely worth reading.**"

"**I reread this book every summer** to prepare myself for the new year."

"This book is **a great resource** for new teachers and veteran teachers."

"It **works wonderfully** for teachers in classrooms **from preschool to middle school!**"

"This program **really works.**"

"**Wonderful resource** for school personnel when working with parents and in the classroom."

"What a great book! **It's amazing how quickly it works.**"

"This is a **great no-nonsense tool** to use in the classroom."

What parents are saying about *1-2-3 Magic*:

"This book **changed our lives**."

"My three-year-old has become a different little girl, **and she is so much happier now**."

"**The ideas in this book work!** It really is like magic! I feel like **I am back in charge**."

"Simple, clear, concise, and **easy to follow**."

"**I highly recommend this book** if you need a method of dealing with your little one(s) that keeps everyone calm."

"Extremely **helpful and informative**."

"A **great book** for any parent!"

"**I was desperate for a change** in my family dynamics. **This book was the answer!**"

"**Fantastic book** that really helps with toddler tantrums. **My husband and I both read it** and now **we are disciplining in the same way**. This book has been a **lifesaver!**"

"*1-2-3 Magic* **simplifies everything** I've read in other books, which makes it **very easy to follow**. Our home has become **a much more positive place**."

"**Easy to read** and easy to follow."

"**Buy this book; read this book; follow the instructions in this book!** I highly recommend this to anyone involved in disciplining children."

1-2-3 MAGIC

in the Classroom

1-2-3 MAGIC

in the Classroom

Effective Discipline for Pre-K through Grade 8

Second Edition

THOMAS W. PHELAN, PhD
SARAH JANE SCHONOUR, MA

 sourcebooks

Published by Sourcebooks, Inc.
P.O. Box 4410, Naperville, Illinois 60567-4410
(630) 961-3900
Fax: (630) 961-2168
www.sourcebooks.com

Originally published as *1-2-3 Magic for Teachers* in 2004 by ParentMagic, Inc.

Library of Congress Cataloging-in-Publication Data

Names: Phelan, Thomas W., author. | Schonour, Sarah Jane, author.
Title: 1-2-3 magic in the classroom : effective discipline for pre-K through grade 8 / Thomas W. Phelan, PhD, and Sarah Jane Schonour, MA.
Description: Second edition. | Naperville, Illinois : Sourcebooks, Inc., 2016. | Includes index.
Identifiers: LCCN 2015050122 | (pbk. : alk. paper)
Subjects: LCSH: Classroom management.
Classification: LCC LB3013 .P455 2016 | DDC 371.102/4--dc23 LC record available at http://lccn.loc.gov/2015050122

Printed and bound in the United States of America.
VP 10 9 8 7 6 5 4 3 2 1

CONTENTS

Preface   xi

Introduction: Teaching: Not for the Faint of Heart!   xv

Part I: Building a Solid Foundation for Classroom Discipline   1

Chapter 1: What Is 1-2-3 Magic?   3

Chapter 2: Identifying Start Behavior and Stop Behavior   7

Chapter 3: Challenging the Little Adult Assumption   12

Chapter 4: Avoiding the Two Biggest Discipline Mistakes   16

Chapter 5: Which Type of Teacher Are You?   20

**Part II: Managing Undesirable Behavior: Classroom
Discipline Step 1**   27

Chapter 6: Getting Results through Counting   29

Chapter 7: Advice for Nearly Any Counting Challenge   42

Chapter 8: How to Handle Peer Conflicts, Pouting, and Tantrums   57

Chapter 9: Getting Started with Counting   62

Part III: Managing Testing and Manipulation   69

Chapter 10: Recognizing the Six Kinds of Testing
and Manipulation   71

Chapter 11: Tales from the Trenches   84

Chapter 12: More Serious Offenses   95

Part IV: Encouraging Good Behavior:
Classroom Discipline Step 2   107

Chapter 13: Establishing Positive Routines   109

Chapter 14: Using 1-2-3 Magic When Your Class Is
    on the Move   129

Chapter 15: Coordinating Arrival, Dismissal, and Transitions   140

Chapter 16: Completing Classroom Jobs and Chores   145

Chapter 17: Getting the Schoolwork Done   149

Chapter 18: Conducting Class Meetings   156

Chapter 19: Discussing Behavior Issues with Your Students   161

Part V: Strengthening Your Relationships with Your Students:
Classroom Discipline Step 3   169

Chapter 20: Utilizing Praise, Fun, and Forgiveness   171

Chapter 21: How to Practice Sympathetic Listening   176

Chapter 22: Working Collaboratively with Parents   186

Part VI: Tips for Using 1-2-3 Magic at Different Grade Levels   191

Chapter 23: Preschool and Day Care   193

Chapter 24: Elementary Grades   201

Chapter 25: Middle School   205

Chapter 26: A Note about Students with Special Needs   216

Part VII: Collaborating with Administrators   225

Chapter 27: Administrative Policy and Teacher Support   227

Chapter 28: Teacher Self-Evaluation Checklist   237

Part VIII: Looking Forward   245

Chapter 29: Enjoying Your New Classroom   247

Appendix   252

Index   257

About the Authors   265

PREFACE

THE VERY FIRST SEMINAR for *1-2-3 Magic: Effective Discipline for Children 2–12* took place at a local Holiday Inn on a cold April day in 1984. It was attended by twenty-eight parents and a few teachers. Since that day, millions of parents, teachers, teacher aides, school administrators, grandparents, camp counselors, therapists, mental health professionals, and pediatricians have used 1-2-3 Magic to solve child discipline issues. Many more adults have learned the program through our books, videos, and audios, and our unit sales have crossed the 1.6 million mark. We now have Leader Guides for parents and for teachers, Spanish books and videos, and more than twenty foreign translations.

The reasons for the success of 1-2-3 Magic are simple. The program is easy to learn, and it works. You can learn it one day and start it the next. There really is no "magic" involved, but we have had many delighted schoolteachers and parents swear that the 1-2-3 program works "like magic." And now, after all these years, we are hearing from people who raised and taught their children—from the ground up—on *1-2-3 Magic*, and these folks often thank us for turning their lives around.

At ParentMagic, Inc., we want to make a dramatic and positive difference in the lives of the people who use our program. We want teachers to have energetic but orderly classrooms where children learn to respect one another and respect their instructors. We want moms and dads to enjoy their children, and to be able to discipline their kids with gentleness, firmness, and decisiveness. We want children to grow up happy, competent, and able to get along with others.

Why an Edition for Teachers?

There are some important distinctions between how a parent would implement 1-2-3 Magic and how a teacher might use the program. As far as we know, few parents have to simultaneously manage the behavior of twenty-five children. Therefore, at the request of many teachers, we developed a book with a school and classroom focus. In writing this book, we have had a great deal of valuable assistance from experienced educators. Special thanks are due to our contributing writers, consultants, and reviewers: Cristina Dougherty (chapter 25), Becky Ferguson (chapter 23), Susan Kernan (chapter 27), Cheryl Hauser, Megan Law, and Shilpi Patel. The contributions and feedback of these individuals are deeply appreciated.

Like the 1-2-3 Magic parenting program, *1-2-3 Magic in the Classroom* organizes the classroom discipline strategy into three separate and critical steps:

1. Managing undesirable behavior
2. Encouraging good behavior
3. Strengthening your relationship with students

These three steps are, of course, interdependent, and they are dealt with in this book in the order above.

Keep in mind, though, the fundamental concept of preventive discipline in the classroom: **a student who is doing his work will not be a behavior problem.** As much as possible, effective teachers structure work, engage students in learning, and monitor progress so that the need for corrective discipline is minimal.

How to Use This Book

1-2-3 Magic in the Classroom describes some straightforward and very effective methods for managing the school behavior of children from the ages of approximately two to fourteen. To get the best results, keep in mind the following:

1. The methods should be used exactly as they are described here, especially with regard to the No Talking and No Emotion rules.
2. If there is more than one adult in the classroom on a regular basis, both adults should use the techniques described.
3. At times, it may be helpful for teachers to get parents and families involved in using the 1-2-3 Magic program. Grandparents, babysitters, and other caregivers have also found the 1-2-3 Magic program very helpful in managing young children. In addition, these days more and more grandparents are raising their grandchildren themselves, and a teacher's suggestion of the program may be a lifesaver for these older adults.
4. Note that illness, allergies, and physical pain can cause and aggravate behavioral and emotional difficulties in children. A teacher may want to ask the parents about any health issues that may affect their child.

Psychological Evaluation and Counseling

Teachers should not make diagnoses regarding the psychological health of their students. However, we encourage a dialogue among teachers, parents, school psychologists, and others regarding the well-being of any child. In fact, the 1-2-3 Magic program can assist teachers in deciding when it might be time to discuss with a parent the possibility of a referral to a school psychologist, school social worker, or special services team.

We hope *1-2-3 Magic in the Classroom* helps you establish the kind of classroom environment you want and—equally important—allows you to look forward to each day at school with your students.

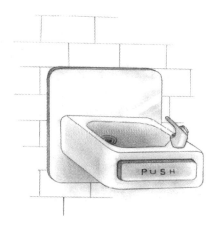

INTRODUCTION

Teaching: Not for the Faint of Heart!

"CAN I GET A DRINK?"

"Not right now."

"Why not?"

"Because we're going to lunch in five minutes. We'll stop for water then."

"But I want a drink now."

"I just told you to wait five minutes."

"You never let me do anything."

"What!? Of course I do. You've been line leader all week."

"You let José get a drink."

"Do you have to do everything José does? Besides, *he* finished his work."

"I promise I'll do all my work."

"I've heard that before. Look at your folder! It's full of unfinished work."

"I'm going to tell my parents!"

"Fine. Be my guest!"

Good Teaching Involves Good Discipline

The only people who think teaching is easy are those who have never taught. Like parenting, this task is one of the most important jobs in the world, but it is not an easy one. Working with young children can be one of life's most enjoyable experiences, yet it can also become unbelievably frustrating.

Educators with romantic notions about teaching often forget that it is impossible for all the children in your classroom to like you and what you are doing. Educating children means that, in addition to nurturing and supporting them, you must also frustrate them on a regular basis—for their own good and for the good of everyone. "Now it's time to get to work. Now you must take a test. Stop teasing your friend. No, you can't get a drink of water." Over and over, firmness and gentleness are required.

Unfortunately, when they are frustrated, kids do not usually thank their teachers for trying to discipline them properly. Instead, youngsters have an amazing natural ability to confuse, sidetrack, and aggravate the adults whom the kids see as responsible for their current distress. We call this "testing and manipulation," and there are six basic types (chapter 10). Testing and manipulation can interfere with learning, eliminate fun, ruin relationships, and destroy a classroom atmosphere.

Repeat the "Drink of Water" scene above a thousand times, and you have guaranteed misery for both teacher and child. That's no way for anyone to spend their time at school, and that is also why a teacher must have a discipline plan ready at the beginning of the year to prevent discipline problems before they start.

Teaching vs. Parenting: Two Big Differences

Teaching is different from parenting in two major ways. First of all, most parents have two or three kids at home, while most teachers have about twenty-five in their classroom.

In addition to having more kids, teachers are not allowed "downtime" with their students. At home, parents can say, "Do whatever you want for a while" to their young charges. In the classroom, however, teachers have to see to it that the learning and work get done—all day long. Even "free time" and recess require adult monitoring.

So classroom teachers have a specific job to do—assigning schoolwork and promoting learning—with lots of children all day long. The chief priority in the classroom, therefore, is getting that work done—not behavioral discipline. It is true that a good discipline plan, such as *1-2-3 Magic in the Classroom*, has both preventive strategies as well as intervention tactics for times when problems pop up. But the fact of the matter remains that a student who is doing his work will not be a discipline problem. Effective teaching—which is not the scope of this book—is the best preventive discipline strategy.[1]

Because adults and kids are not perfect, however, the best teaching still requires an effective discipline plan to back it up. That's why there is a program like 1-2-3 Magic. Adults need to know how to handle difficult behavior, encourage good behavior, and manage the inevitable sidetrack of testing and manipulation—all in a manner that is fair, perfectly clear, and not abusive. When children's inevitable troublesome behaviors are handled in routine and successful ways, the more productive side of the teacher-student relationship is allowed to kick in. Learning, praise, conscientious work, and shared fun can flow naturally. Good discipline, in other words, makes for better teaching and for good times.

> **Key Concept**
>
> A student who is doing his work will not be a discipline problem. Effective teaching is the best preventive discipline strategy.

1-2-3: Three Steps to Effective Discipline

1-2-3 Magic in the Classroom will provide you with three steps for effective discipline. Each of the three steps is distinct, manageable, and

---

1. Perhaps the best guide to the effective-teaching part of the classroom equation is Harry K. Wong and Rosemary T. Wong's classic, *The First Days of School: How to Be an Effective Teacher*.

extremely important. The three steps are also mutually interdependent; in other words, each one depends to some extent on the others for its success.

- **Step 1** involves *managing undesirable behavior*. No teacher will get along well with her students if the children are constantly irritating her with whining, arguing, teasing, badgering, tantrums, yelling, and fighting. In *1-2-3 Magic in the Classroom*, you will learn how to "count" obnoxious behavior to motivate children to stop, and you will be pleasantly surprised at how effective that simple technique is!
- **Step 2** involves *encouraging good behavior*. Encouraging good behavior, such as cleaning up, transitioning, being courteous, and doing classwork, takes more effort—for both adult and child—than managing difficult behavior. You will learn seven simple methods to help encourage positive actions in your kids.
- **Step 3** involves learning some valuable and not-so-difficult ways of *strengthening your relationships with your students*. Some teachers merely need to be reminded of these strategies; other teachers have to work hard at them. Paying attention to the quality of your relationships with the children in your class will help you with steps 1 and 2, and vice versa.

Let's get going. And good luck!

CHAPTER SUMMARY

The three steps to effective discipline are:

1. Managing undesirable behavior
2. Encouraging good behavior
3. Strengthening your relationships with your students

⦚⦚⦚⦚ PART I ⦚⦚⦚⦚

Building a Solid Foundation for Classroom Discipline

CHAPTER 1
What Is 1-2-3 Magic?

CHAPTER 2
Identifying Start Behavior and Stop Behavior

CHAPTER 3
Challenging the Little Adult Assumption

CHAPTER 4
Avoiding the Two Biggest Discipline Mistakes

CHAPTER 5
Which Type of Teacher Are You?

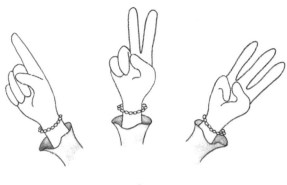

1

WHAT IS 1-2-3 MAGIC?

An Explanation of Our Effective, Simple Discipline Program

THE 1-2-3 MAGIC PROGRAM is not magic. Instead, it is a simple, precise, and effective way of gently and firmly managing the behavior of children from approximately the preschool years through eighth grade. The reason for our unusual title is that so many teachers, parents, and other child caretakers have said, "It works like magic!" *1-2-3 Magic in the Classroom* certainly does work if you use the program correctly, which means following a few simple, basic rules. The 1-2-3 program is what you might call a "teacher-in-charge" strategy, but no arguing, yelling, or negative physical contact is allowed.

Teaching Behavior As Well As Academics

Many teachers feel well prepared to teach academics to their students, yet very much *unprepared* to address challenging behavior. It is difficult—if not impossible—to teach a group of students who are out of control; undesirable behavior must be managed if any learning is to occur. The trouble is that many teachers do not know where to start with behavior management. They may have had parts of one or two classes at the university level that addressed this subject, but they are still unsure of how to utilize their limited information to maintain control in their classrooms.

In the very first days of the school year, students quickly sense whether their instructor has a decisive and calm strategy for behavior management. Weak and uncertain strategies make many students anxious, while they allow other children to act up more and thus disrupt the learning environment. Yet it is critical to the success of teacher and students to have a safe and calm classroom. This is where *1-2-3 Magic in the Classroom* comes in.

The method described in this book is easy to master, and you can start the program right away. Too many discipline programs start by pointing out the approximately fifty discipline mistakes you are supposedly making in your classroom at the present time. Then, in the hope of helping you to correct these errors, the program presents fifty elaborate strategies that require an advanced degree in educational psychology in order to be able to use them properly. The result? You are left with bad feelings, confusion, and no clear place to start. Worse than that, things in your classroom stay the same or get worse.

After reading *1-2-3 Magic in the Classroom*, however, you will know exactly what to do, what not to do, what to say, and what not to say in just about every one of the common, everyday problem situations you run into with your students. Because *1-2-3 Magic in the Classroom* is based on only a few basic but critical principles, *you will also be able to remember what to do, and you will be able to do it when you are anxious, agitated, or upset.* You will also be able to be a kind but effective teacher when you are busy, in a hurry, or otherwise

> ### Key Concept
> Many teachers feel well prepared to teach academics to their students, but very much unprepared to address challenging behavior. It is difficult—if not impossible—to teach a group of students who are out of control.

preoccupied. In addition to managing minor but frequent problems, you will also know how to handle more serious behavior issues, such as lying, stealing, and fighting.

You will find that if you use the 1-2-3 program correctly, it will work! 1-2-3 Magic has been shown to be very effective with two- to fourteen-year-old students, whether they are children with special needs or typically developing youngsters. In fact, 1-2-3 Magic has been used successfully with children with learning disabilities, attention deficit disorder, emotional disabilities, and visual and hearing impairments. It has also been used with children with developmental disabilities and/or intellectual disabilities. To benefit properly from the 1-2-3 program, the only rule is that a child must have a cognitive age of at least two years.

When you finish learning about the 1-2-3 Magic program, it is a good idea to start using it immediately. Talk with any instructional teammates you may have, and then get going right away.

If you are in your classroom on your own, take a deep breath and explain the 1-2-3 program to your students. Also send a letter home and have a parent night when you show all your parents and families part of the *1-2-3 Magic* parent video. A picture is worth a thousand words, and after seeing the video (especially the Famous Twinkie Example), many of your parents will want to start using the program at home. The resulting school/home cooperation and consistency are often worth their weight in gold, especially with children with unusually difficult behavior.

If you are a school counselor or social worker, you may suggest that parents or teachers get a copy of the *1-2-3 Magic* book at their local bookstore, or you can provide them with a copy of the *1-2-3 Magic* video. The Parent Teacher Association (PTA) may also want to have these items available for checkout.

What to Expect When You Begin the 1-2-3 Program

When you do start *1-2-3 Magic in the Classroom*, things will change quickly. Initially, the majority of your students will fall into the "immediate cooperator" category. You start the program, and they cooperate right away—sometimes "just like magic." What do you do? Just relax and enjoy your good fortune!

A few of the kids, however, might fall into the "immediate tester" category. The behavior of these children gets worse first. They challenge you to see if you really mean business with your new ideas and methods. If you stick to your guns, however—no arguing, yelling, or physical intimidation—you will get these little testers shaped up pretty well in about a week to ten days. Then what do you do? You start enjoying your students again.

Believe it or not, you may soon have a much more peaceful classroom and more enjoyable kids. You will be less exhausted by having to discipline, and you will have more time for instruction.

CHAPTER SUMMARY

Once you start using 1-2-3 Magic, your students will fall into one of two categories:

1. Immediate cooperators (the majority)
2. Immediate testers (a few)

Enjoy the cooperators and brace yourself for the testers!

2

IDENTIFYING START BEHAVIOR AND STOP BEHAVIOR

How Understanding Two Types of Behavior Will Solve Your Discipline Problems

THERE ARE TWO BASIC kinds of problems that students present to their teachers. When you are frustrated with your students, the children are either (1) doing something you want them to *stop*, or (2) *not* doing something you would like them to *start*. In the 1-2-3 Magic program, therefore, we call these two kinds of things "Stop" behavior and "Start" behavior. In the hustle and bustle of everyday existence, you may not have worried much about the difference between Stop and Start behaviors, but—as we'll soon see—the distinction is extremely important.

Stop behavior includes the frequent, minor, everyday problem behaviors that kids present, such as whining, disrespecting, talking out of turn, arguing, teasing, pouting, yelling, and getting out of one's seat. Stop behavior—in and of itself—ranges from mildly irritating to obnoxious. Each of these difficult behaviors may not be so bad on its own, but add them all up in one afternoon, and by 3:00 p.m. you may feel like hitchhiking to South America.

Start behavior, on the other hand, includes constructive activities like cleaning up, doing work, practicing facts, transitioning from one activity to another, raising one's hand, and being nice to other people. When you have a problem with Start behavior, your student is not doing something that, in your eyes, would be a good thing to do. It's important to distinguish between Stop and Start behaviors because you will use different tactics for each kind of problem.

For **Stop** behavior problems, such as:

Whining

Disrespecting

Talking out of turn

Teasing

Arguing

Pouting

Yelling

Getting out of one's seat

Use the 1-2-3, or "counting," procedure.
Counting is simple, gentle, and direct.

For **Start** behavior problems, such as:

Cleaning up

Doing work

Raising one's hand

Choose from several tactics, which can be used either singly or in combination. These tactics include praise, simple requests, kitchen timers, the docking system, natural consequences, charting, cross dialogue, and the counting variation. Start behavior strategies, as you can probably guess, require more thought and effort than counting does.

Why the difference in strategies? The answer lies in the issue of motivation. How long does it take a child—if she is motivated—to terminate a Stop behavior like screaming or being disrespectful? The answer is about one second; it's really not a big project. And—depending on how angry or oppositional a child is—terminating an occurrence of obnoxious behavior doesn't take tons of effort.

But now look at Start behavior. How long does it take a child to eat lunch? Maybe twenty to twenty-five minutes. To clean his desk? Perhaps fifteen minutes. To get ready for dismissal? Ten to fifteen minutes. How about completing a geography assignment? This might take anywhere from thirty minutes to three years. So it's obvious that with Start behavior, more motivation is required from the child. He has to begin the project, keep at it, and then finish it. And the project is often something he is not thrilled about having to do in the first place.

In addition, if engaging in positive behavior in kids requires more motivation in the kids, it's also going to require more motivation from the instructor. As you'll soon see, putting an end to Stop behavior using counting is relatively easy if you do it right. Start behavior requires more sophisticated tactics.

When managing a behavioral difficulty with one of your pupils, therefore, you will need to first determine if you have a Stop or a Start behavior problem. Is the issue something you want the child to quit? Or is it something you want him or her to get going on? Since counting is so easy, one of the biggest problems we run into is adults mistakenly using counting for Start behavior; for example, counting a child to get her to do her schoolwork. As you will soon see, counting produces motivation in children that usually lasts only a short time (from a few seconds to a couple of minutes) and does not provide the lasting motivation needed to get a child to continue desired behavior. If you mix up your tactics (e.g., use counting for schoolwork), you will not get optimum results.

Pop Quiz!

Just for practice, take this short Stop behavior vs. Start behavior quiz.

1. Anna is whining about wanting to share her Show and Tell immediately. **Stop or Start?**
2. Seth does not begin working when the other students do. **Stop or Start?**
3. Karen drops her coat on the floor inside the doorway and then goes to her desk. **Stop or Start?**
4. James tells another student that she's stupid. **Stop or Start?**
5. Tammy bursts into the classroom and yells, "It's snowing outside!" **Stop or Start?**

How did you do? The answers are:

1. **Stop**
2. **Start**
3. **Start**
4. **Stop**
5. **Stop**

You're probably aware by now that some problems have both Stop and Start behavior aspects to them. If Johnny is talking to his neighbor (a Stop behavior), he cannot also be doing his math (a Start behavior).

Don't worry. The 1-2-3 Magic procedure is so simple, you'll be an expert in no time. Effective discipline will start to come naturally and—believe it or not—your students will start listening to you.

CHAPTER SUMMARY:

For **Stop** behavior, such as:

Talking
Disrespecting
Arguing
Teasing
Yelling
Getting out of seat

 Use the 1-2-3, or "counting," procedure.

For **Start** behavior, such as:

Cleaning up
Doing your work
Raising your hand
Transitioning
Listening

 Use praise, simple requests, kitchen timers, the docking system, natural consequences, charting, the counting variation, and cross dialogue.

3

CHALLENGING THE LITTLE ADULT ASSUMPTION

Why You Need to Remember That Kids Are Just Kids

MANY TEACHERS AND PARENTS carry around in their heads an enchanting but trouble-producing notion about young children. This idea is a kind of false assumption or wish that produces discipline attempts that don't work, along with stormy scenes that make everyone feel bad. This erroneous concept is known as the "Little Adult Assumption."

The Little Adult Assumption is the belief that kids are basically reasonable and unselfish. In other words, they're just smaller versions of grown-ups. This notion goes on to imply that because they are little adults, whenever the youngsters are misbehaving or not cooperating, the problem must be that they don't have enough information at their disposal to be able to do the right thing. The solution? Simply give them the facts.

Imagine, for example, that one of your third-grade students is teasing her peer for the fifteenth time since they arrived at school. What should you do? If your student were a little adult, you would simply sit her down, calmly look her in the eye, and explain to her the three golden reasons why she shouldn't tease her friend. First of all, teasing hurts the other child. Second, it makes you irritated with the girl doing the teasing. Third—and most important—how would she feel if someone treated her like that?

Imagine further that your student then looks at you, her face brightening with insight, and she says, "Gee, I never looked at it like that before!" Then she stops bothering her classmate for the rest of the year. That would certainly be nice, but any veteran teacher knows that doesn't happen. Kids are not little adults.

The crucial point here is this: Grown-ups who believe the Little Adult Assumption are going to rely heavily on *words and reasons* in dealing with kids and trying to change their behavior. And words and reasons, by themselves, are going to be miserable failures much of the time. Sometimes explanations will have absolutely no impact at all. Other times, explanations will take the teacher and child through what we call the Talk-Persuade-Argue-Yell-Hit syndrome.

Quick Tip

Adults who want to believe in the Little Adult Assumption are going to rely heavily on words and reasons to change kids' behavior. But words and reasons are going to be miserable failures much of the time.

Imagine this: your student is doing something you don't like. You read in a book that you should talk the problem out no matter how long it takes. So you try telling your student why she shouldn't be doing what she's doing. She doesn't respond, so you next try to persuade her to see things your way. When persuasion fails, you start arguing with the little girl. Arguing leads to a yelling match, and when that fails, you are at the end of your rope.

Actually, the vast majority of the time, when an adult screams at a child, the *adult* is simply having a temper tantrum. The tantrum is a sign that (1) the adult doesn't know what to do, (2) the adult is so frustrated that he or she can't see straight, or (3) this adult may have an anger management problem.

As we'll clarify later, talking and explaining certainly have their place in educating children. But kids are just kids—not little adults. Years ago one writer said, "Childhood is a period of transitory psychosis." She meant that when kids are little, they are sort of nuts! They are not born reasonable and unselfish; they are born unreasonable and selfish. Consequently, it is the parent's job—and the teacher's job—to help kids become the opposite. In accomplishing this goal, adults need to be gentle, consistent, decisive, and calm.

How do you do that? You start by changing your thinking about children and by getting rid of the Little Adult Assumption. In order to get this erroneous notion out of adults' heads, we use a bit of what we call "cognitive shock." Although it's a little exaggerated and may sound strange, think of it like this: instead of imagining your students as little adults, think of yourself as a wild animal trainer! Of course, we don't mean using whips or chairs. And we certainly don't mean being nasty.

> **Caution**
>
> One explanation, if really necessary, is fine. It's the attempts at repeated explanations that get adults and kids into trouble. Too much explaining and talking irritates and distracts children.

But what does a wild animal trainer do? He chooses a method—which is firm, gentle, and largely nonverbal—and repeats it until the "trainee" does what he, the trainer, wants. The trainer is patient and kind, positive and persistent. Our job in *1-2-3 Magic in the Classroom* is to present some useful training methods to you, so that you can repeat them until the trainees—your students—do what you want them to do.

Fortunately, you do not usually have to repeat these methods for very long before you get results. And you can gradually add more talking and reasoning into your strategy with older students. But remember this: one explanation—if necessary—is fine. It's the attempts at repeated explanations that get teachers and children in trouble.

Being a Teacher in Charge

The overall orientation of 1-2-3 Magic is that the teacher is the one who is in charge of the classroom. The classroom is not a democracy. Unfortunately, some teachers these days seem to be almost afraid of their pupils. What are they afraid of? Physical attack? Not usually. What many teachers fear is that their students won't like them. So, in conflict situations, these teachers explain and explain and explain, hoping the children will eventually come around. All too often, however, these wordy efforts simply lead to the Talk-Persuade-Argue-Yell-Hit syndrome.

> **Key Concept**
>
> Noncompliance and lack of cooperation are not always due to lack of information. Kids are not little adults or simply small computers, so teaching youngsters involves training as well as explaining.

What if you have students who always respond to words and reasons? You are certainly lucky! If you have a classroom full of them, you may not need this book. On the other hand, if you don't have students like this—or if your students stop responding to logic—you can consider using the 1-2-3 program.

So what is this training method we're talking about? We first have to explain what it is not.

CHAPTER SUMMARY

What's wrong with this picture?

GEE, I NEVER LOOKED AT IT LIKE THAT BEFORE! THANKS FOR THE EXPLANATION.

4

AVOIDING THE TWO BIGGEST DISCIPLINE MISTAKES

The Dangers of Too Much Talking and Too Much Emotion

THE TWO BIGGEST MISTAKES that teachers make when trying to discipline children are these: too much talking and too much emotion. Thinking of kids as little adults and then engaging in excessive explaining during a situation that requires discipline makes kids less likely to cooperate by irritating, confusing, and distracting them. Endless chatter also leads to the Talk-Persuade-Argue-Yell-Hit syndrome.

Why is too much emotion destructive? Don't people today tell you to "let it all hang out" and show your feelings? "Express yourself and don't keep it all inside" seems to be the universal recommendation of modern psychology.

Is this a good suggestion if you are working with children? One-half of it is good advice, and the other half is not. The good half is this: if you are feeling positively toward a child, let it show. Praise your students for their constructive and conscientious behavior and give them a pat on the shoulder.

The bad half of the don't-keep-it-all-inside advice, though, applies to times when you are irritated or angry with a child. Cutting loose at these moments can be a problem, because when adults are mad, we often do the wrong thing. Angry adults can yell, scream, belittle, and nag. 1-2-3 Magic is as much a control on adult anger as it is a control on children's behavior.

There is another reason why too much emotion can interfere with effective teaching. When they are little, kids feel inferior to adults. They feel inferior because they *are* inferior. They are smaller, less privileged, less intelligent, less skillful, less responsible, and less of just about everything than adults and older kids. And this "lessness" bugs them a lot. They don't like it. They like to feel they are powerful and capable of making some mark on the world.

> **Key Concept**
>
> If you have a pupil who is doing something you don't like, get very upset about it on a regular basis, and—sure enough—she'll repeat it for you!

If you watch two-year-olds, you will see that they want to be like the five-year-olds, who can do more neat things. The five-year-olds, in turn, want to be like the ten-year-olds. And the ten-year-olds want to be like you; they want to drive cars and use credit cards! They want to have some impact on the world and to make things happen.

Have you ever seen a small child go down to a lake and throw rocks in the water? Children can do that for hours, partly because the big splashes are a sign of their impact. They are the ones causing all the commotion.

What does throwing rocks in the water have to do with what happens in school? Simple. If your little pupil can get you all upset, *your upset is the big splash for him.* Your emotional outburst has the unintended consequence of making that child feel powerful. His reaction does not mean that he has no conscience or that he is going to grow up to be a professional criminal. It's just a normal childhood feeling: having all that power temporarily rewards—or feels good to—the part of the child that feels inferior. Teachers who say, "It drives me absolutely crazy when she taps her pencil constantly! Why does she do that?" may have already answered the question. She may do that—at least partly—*because it drives the teachers crazy.*

An important rule, therefore, is this: if you have a child who is doing something you don't like, get very upset about it on a regular basis and,

> ## Key Concept
> You get more of what you pay attention to—so be sure to acknowledge good behavior.

sure enough, she'll repeat it for you. You will get more of what you pay attention to, so it is important to minimize the attention paid to negative behavior and maximize the attention paid to positive behavior.

During moments involving conflict or discipline, you want to be consistent, decisive, and calm. So what we recommend in 1-2-3 Magic is that you apply what we call the "No Talking" and "No Emotion" rules. Since we're all human, these two rules actually mean "very little talking" and "very little emotion." *But these rules are absolutely critical to your disciplinary effectiveness.* There are discipline systems other than the 1-2-3 program, but you will ruin any of them by talking too much or getting too excited. These two mistakes, of course, usually go hand in hand, and the emotion involved is usually anger.

Some teachers can turn off the talking and the emotional upset like a faucet, especially once they see how effective it is to keep quiet at the right times. Other adults need to practice looking bored or disinterested when their kids are acting up. And still other adults have to ferociously bite their tongues to get the job done. We once saw a T-shirt that had this printed on the front: "Help me—I'm talking and I can't stop!" Lots of teachers have to remind themselves over and over and over again that talking, arguing, yelling, and screaming actually make things worse in the classroom. These "tactics" merely blow off steam for a few seconds. If, after a month to six weeks of using 1-2-3 Magic, you find that you can't shake these troublesome habits, it may be time for a friendly consultation with the school psychologist, a social worker, or an outside therapist.

CHAPTER SUMMARY

Too Much Talking
Too Much Emotion

5

WHICH TYPE OF TEACHER ARE YOU?

How Your Personality and Teaching Style Affect Your Students

A WELL-MANAGED, POSITIVE CLASSROOM environment starts with the teacher. If things are going well, the teacher should congratulate herself. If things are not going smoothly, this fact is a message to the teacher that it's time to look in the mirror to see what she could be doing differently. Certainly, "it takes two to tango"— students are an integral part of the classroom, and they have their own responsibilities. However, the ongoing process of maintaining a calm and productive classroom starts with the adult.

This idea fits nicely with our No Talking and No Emotion rules. The actions and attitudes of a teacher toward a student who is misbehaving can make the situation better or worse. Have you ever noticed that on a day that you are not feeling well, the students are more poorly behaved? Students look to the teacher for consistency and safety in the classroom. Some kids will become anxious and withdrawn if it appears that a teacher cannot handle behavior problems. Other students, however, will retaliate if they feel a teacher is overreacting to a situation in a hostile and unnecessary way.

Teachers manifest many different personality and teaching styles in the classroom, and it is sometimes helpful to categorize these educational approaches in terms of some very basic dimensions. It has often been said that good teachers (as well as good parents) are both warm and demanding. Being warm means showing caring and emotional support for students. Being demanding—in the good sense—means expecting something from your kids, both in terms of academic work and behavior. Depending on whether the warm and demanding switches are in the OFF or ON position, we can describe four fundamental teaching styles:

Authoritarian: demanding switch ON; warm switch OFF

Permissive: demanding switch OFF; warm switch ON

Detached: demanding switch OFF; warm switch OFF

Authoritative: demanding switch ON; warm switch ON

Although these categories are generalizations, and few adults will neatly fit into any one type all the time, these concepts can be very useful when it comes to teacher evaluation and remediation. Let's look briefly at each.

The Four Categories of Teaching Styles

Authoritarian: Demanding ON, Warm OFF

Typically, teachers in this category are quick to "jump" on each and every behavior that is not acceptable in the classroom. Warmth, support, and positive reinforcement, however, are rare. The authoritarian teacher may use a loud voice to get the attention of her students. She

is very demanding and expects her students to follow the rules because it is "the right thing to do." She may act shocked and angry when students don't follow her directives. The "benefit" of this style is that the teacher frequently gets immediate compliance from her students.

What is the cost of the authoritarian style? The risks include student anxiety and minimal long-term positive effects. No student enjoys a teacher's yelling and screaming. Although the kids may comply out of fear, this teaching technique rarely produces behavioral changes that last over time. An authoritarian teacher using this style may find that she is constantly "on" her students to behave, which can lead to the teacher blaming the students for the problems in the class.

Permissive: Demanding OFF, Warm ON

Teachers in this category are often "too nice." They want the students to like them, and they want to be helpful, so they are warm and supportive but not very good at setting limits. Permissive teachers may focus primarily on effort while de-emphasizing the quality of students' productions. Irritating or disruptive behaviors such as talking, being out of one's seat, getting out of line, and not raising one's hand may be ignored or handled with weak, soft-spoken "reprimands" or pleading.

While warmth and support are admirable qualities, students appreciate discipline, even if they don't show it. The cost of this teaching style is a classroom that is out of control. Constructive learning does not flow well. While students may describe this teacher as "nice and easy," when push comes to shove, they do not feel that they can trust her to

Key Concept

While students may describe a permissive teacher as "nice and easy," when push comes to shove, they do not feel that they can trust her to take care of problem situations.

take care of problem situations. Students may feel that they need to take situations into their own hands because if they tell the teacher, she will not do anything. Other students may just get more nervous, waiting for the next crisis. The permissive teacher herself will also feel anxious a good deal because she is not sure what to do when a student misbehaves, and she worries that other teachers may view her as a "pushover."

Detached: Demanding OFF, Warm OFF

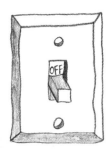

The detached teacher tends to be neither warm nor demanding. She may sit at her desk when students are working or grade papers when "supervising" the playground. Pupils who need extra emotional support do not get it from her, and pupils who need firm behavioral limits do not get that either. The detached type of teacher just does not seem particularly concerned about the behavior or the academic production of her students. The detached style may at times result from an extremely low energy level because of physical illness or depression. On the other hand, the detached approach may reflect a basic and pervasive lack of knowledge and skill about exactly how to be warm and demanding.

The costs of this style are significant. The detached teacher may miss important "warning signs" from students who are having trouble, either academically or behaviorally. Other students may withdraw and feel unimportant because they are receiving no positive reinforcement for what they do. And still other kids may increase acting-out behavior in order to get the teacher's attention or simply because there is no control in the classroom for their wayward energies. All these factors will limit the total amount of learning that takes place.

Authoritative: Demanding ON, Warm ON

The authoritative teacher is obviously the ideal, though this approach is easier said than done! This teacher has a positive, kind, and supportive relationship with her students, but they know when she

"means business." Because she has an effective discipline plan and her classroom is orderly, the students trust and respect her. There is more time for academics in this classroom because the students know the expectations of the teacher, and the consequences for misbehavior are consistent. This teacher also feels empowered and energized because she sees positive growth and development in her students. Her students feel safe as well as capable.

Theoretically, of course, there are no distinct costs associated with the authoritative style, except for the fact that this kind of teaching takes a lot of energy, flexibility (e.g., switching from warm to demanding and back), and experience.

1-2-3 *Magic in the Classroom* and Teaching Style

1-2-3 Magic in the Classroom is intended to represent and define the authoritative teaching approach. If you think back to our three steps to effective teaching, here is how each step stacks up on the warm and demanding model.

Step 1: Managing undesirable behavior
DEMANDING

Step 2: Encouraging good behavior
DEMANDING and WARM

Step 3: Strengthening your relationships with your students
WARM

Counting undesirable behavior, for example, is largely a demanding tactic. Though it should never be done in an angry or harsh manner, counting cannot be described as a warm type of strategy. Encouraging constructive behavior, on the other hand, can be done with tactics that might be perceived as both warm *and* demanding. Across-the-room praise, for instance, is a warm tactic for the child receiving it, but it is a demanding tactic to the child in the neighboring seat (for whom it is really intended) who is not paying attention. Finally, strengthening relationships with one's students involves methods such as shared fun, sympathetic listening, and forgiveness, which fall mostly into the warm category.

This conceptual framework also provides important, clear, and very specific suggestions for teachers whose classroom style needs some work. Authoritarian types, for example, might want to consider using counting instead of yelling or other scare tactics. These individuals might also need to admit that they are deficient in terms of steps 2 and 3. Permissive types, though, might be very good as far as step 3 is concerned and fair as far as step 2 goes. But what permissive teachers really need is a good lesson in counting difficult behavior—laying down the law gently but firmly. Detached types of teachers obviously need help with all three steps, and some of these individuals will also need some physical or psychological assistance in finding a way to deal with the problems that sap their available energy in the first place.

CHAPTER SUMMARY

Take a few minutes to reflect. How would you describe your teaching style?

PART II

Managing Undesirable Behavior

Classroom Discipline Step 1

CHAPTER 6
Getting Results through Counting

CHAPTER 7
Advice for Nearly Any Counting Challenge

CHAPTER 8
How to Handle Peer Conflicts, Pouting, and Tantrums

CHAPTER 9
Getting Started with Counting

6

GETTING RESULTS
THROUGH COUNTING

Sometimes Your Silence Speaks
Louder Than Your Words

WHEN YOUR STUDENTS ARE acting up, you now know what you're not supposed to do: get excited and start chattering. But just what *are* you supposed to do?

To help with your first step—controlling undesirable behavior—you'll use the 1-2-3, or counting, procedure. Counting is surprisingly powerful and deceptively simple, but you have to know what you're doing in order for this process to be most effective. In the beginning, keep two things in mind.

> ♦ First, you will use the counting method to deal with Stop (obnoxious, difficult, or otherwise undesirable) behavior. In other words, you will be counting things like arguing, talking in class, whining, yelling, wandering out of one's area, teasing a classmate, and so on. You will not use the 1-2-3

method to get a child to do her work or to motivate her to practice vocabulary.

♦ Second, if you are new to 1-2-3 Magic, you will be skeptical after you learn how to do the counting procedure. The procedure may seem too easy; it may not appear aggressive or tough enough. Some of you will think, "Hey, you don't know my class. These kids are wild!"

Don't worry about feeling skeptical. Remember, the 1-2-3 program *is* simple, but it is not always easy. The "magic" is not in the counting. Anyone can count. The magic—or what may seem like magic—is in the No Talking and No Emotion rules. Watching you follow these rules makes children think and take responsibility for their own behavior.

Key Concept

The 1-2-3 program *is* simple, but it is not always easy.

Of course, there really is no magic in 1-2-3 Magic—it just seems that way. The program applies the careful, logical, and persistent extension of a special behavioral technology to the gentle discipline and training of your pupils. Soon, when conflicts with kids arise, you will feel like a new person: consistent, decisive, and calm.

Introduction to Counting

How does the 1-2-3 process work? For the purposes of illustration, we're going to borrow an example from the home to start with, and then we'll show how the technique transfers to the classroom.

Some of you have raised preschoolers, so let's imagine you have a four-year-old child. At 5:45 one afternoon, this little boy is having a major temper tantrum on the floor because you—in your hardness of heart—would not give him a bag of chips right before dinner. The child is banging his head on the floor, kicking the wall, and screaming bloody murder. You are sure your neighbors can hear the noise all the way down the street, and you're at a loss as to what to do.

Your pediatrician told you to ignore these temper tantrums, but you don't think you can stand it. Your mother told you to put a cold washcloth on the boy's face, but you think her advice is strange. And, finally, your spouse told you to spank him.

None of these is an acceptable course of action. Instead, you hold up one finger, look down at the noisy little fellow, and calmly say, "That's 1."

He doesn't care. He's insane with rage and keeps his tantrum going full blast. You let five seconds go by, and then you hold up two fingers and say, "That's 2." You get the same lousy reaction; the tantrum continues. So after five more seconds, you hold up three fingers and say, "That's 3, take five."

Now what does all this mean? It means that the child was just given two chances, or warnings—the first two counts—to shape up. But in this instance he blew it—he didn't stop the undesirable behavior. So there is going to be a consequence. The consequence can be a "rest period," or "time-out" (at home, about one minute per year of the child's life), or the consequence can be what we call a "time-out alternative" (loss of a privilege for a period of time, earlier bedtime, no electronic equipment for two hours, and so on).

Let's imagine the consequence you choose is a rest period, or time-out. After you say, "That's 3, take five," the child goes for the rest period. (Teachers may wonder at this point, "What if he won't go?" or "Where should the time-out area be?" Those questions will be answered in just a moment.)

After the time-out is served by the four-year-old in our example, you will not believe what happens next. Nothing! No talking, no emotion, no apologies, no lectures, no discussions. Nothing is said unless it is absolutely necessary, which is usually not the case.

You do not say, for instance, "Now, are you going to be a good boy? Do you realize what you've been doing to me all afternoon? Why do we have to go through this all the

> **Quick Tip**
> What is going to happen, in a very short period of time, is this: you'll get good control—believe it or not—at 1 or 2. And that is going to make you feel really good!

time? I'm so sick and tired of this, I could scream! Now, your sister doesn't behave this way, and your father's coming home in half an hour. Are you trying to drive me crazy!?"

As tempting as this mini-lecture might be, you simply remain quiet. If the child does something else that's countable, count it. If the child behaves, praise him and enjoy his company.

What is going to happen, in a relatively short period of time, is this: you'll start getting good control—believe it or not—at counts 1 or 2. And we will promise you this: the first time you stop an argument or fight between two of your students from across the room by saying, "That's 1" or "That's 2," and you don't have to get up or yell or scream or do something worse that you're going to be sorry about later…the first time you do that, you're going to feel really good!

Some teachers ask, "I have one child who always takes me to 2. He never seems to stop at 1. Don't you think he's manipulating me?" The answer is no. Why? Because what really drives adults crazy is 42! Or 72!—a child who has to be told a thousand times before he'll shape up. Such multiple reprimands are very disruptive to a classroom. Two counts is not so bad, and remember, if the child reaches 3, he pays the consequences.

Other educators ask, with good reason, "What if my student does something that's so bad that I don't want them to have three chances to stop doing it?" That's a good question. For example, what if a child hits another child? This is not allowed. If one child hits another, it would be ridiculous to say, "That's 1," and give him two more chances to slug away. So if in your opinion the behavior is bad enough to begin with, you simply say, "That's 3." The consequence then is going to be a bigger one— either a longer time-out or a larger version of a time-out alternative (e.g., note home, visit to the principal, and so on).

As you can see, counting is extremely

Key Concept

Talk too much and you take your student's focus off the need for good behavior. Instead, you switch the youngster's attention to the possibility of an energetic—and perhaps enjoyable—argument.

simple, direct, and effective. You are thinking that there must be a catch. There is.

Counting Challenges

Occasionally, we have run into a teacher who says, "I went to your workshop about eight weeks ago and enjoyed it. I have several students with challenging behaviors in my class this year. When I tried your 1-2-3 technique, I was very surprised. 1-2-3 Magic worked, and my students were much better behaved. But that was two months ago. The 1-2-3 method is not working anymore. I need a new discipline program."

What's the problem here? Ninety percent of the time, the problem is that the instructor "forgot" the No Talking and No Emotion rules. Adults can slip up like this *without even knowing it*. Remember our parenting example at the beginning of the chapter, with the four-year-old tantrum artist? Here's how that scene might sound if the parent were unwittingly talking too much and getting too excited while attempting to count the child's outburst:

"That's 1… Come on now, I'm getting a little tired of this. Why can't you do one little thing for me—LOOK AT ME WHEN I'M TALKING TO YOU, YOUNG MAN! OK, that's 2. One more and you're out of here…do you hear me? I'm sick and tired of you whining and fussing over every little thing you can't have. One more and that's it. YOUR SISTER NEVER BEHAVES THIS WAY! OK, ENOUGH! THAT'S 3, TAKE FIVE. OUT OF MY SIGHT!"

What was that? That was an adult temper tantrum. Now we have two tantrums going on in the same kitchen. This adult's outburst was not the 1-2-3 program at all. What's wrong with what this furious adult just did? Three things.

First, if you do "communicate" like this parent just did, the translation of what you are saying is really this: "Let's fight!" And you don't have to have a kid with attention deficit disorder (ADD), oppositional defiant disorder (ODD), or conduct disorder (CD) to get a fight. There are plenty of kids who would sooner cut off their left leg than lose a good battle of words. Unwise attempts at talking or persuading are guaranteed to take a child's focus *off* the possibility of good behavior and put it *on* the prospect of an enjoyable and energetic argument.

Second, many children with difficult behavior do have attention-deficit/hyperactivity disorder (ADHD). That doesn't mean they don't get enough attention. It means they can't *pay* attention. How is a child with ADHD, or any other child for that matter, supposed to pick out—from that huge mass of adult words—the most important parts, which are the counts, or warnings? He can't. Children can't respond properly to warnings if they don't receive them clearly in the first place.

> **Quick Tip**
> Children can't respond properly to warnings if they don't receive them clearly in the first place.

Finally, even if you forget all the emotion involved, as adults talk more and more in a discipline situation, their message fundamentally changes. When a teacher or parent gives lots and lots of reasons to a child regarding why he should shape up, the real message becomes: "You don't have to behave unless I can give you five or six good reasons why you should. And, gee whiz, I certainly hope you agree with my reasons." This is no longer discipline. The word describing this "strategy" starts with the letter *b*. It's *begging*. When you beg like this, you are (1) thinking for the child, (2) taking the responsibility for his behavior, and (3) getting caught up in the Little Adult Assumption.

What's the average child going to do? He's often going to take issue with your reasons. "The other kids don't always do what you say." "I'm not bothering anybody." Now you have left the discipline ballpark, and you're out in the street arguing. The main issue—the child's behavior—has been forgotten.

So if a student is acting up, it's "That's 1" (bite your tongue). Then, if necessary, "That's 2" (easy does it, keep quiet), and so on. Remember that the magic is not in the counting; it's in the pregnant pause right after the count. In that moment—if the teacher keeps still—the responsibility for the child's behavior falls squarely on the youngster's own shoulders. You wouldn't want it any other way.

When it comes to counting, your silence will speak louder than your words.

"Can I Get a Drink?"

Our Drink of Water example will help you better understand the workings of the 1-2-3 process. Here is a situation almost all teachers have experienced at one time or another.

> ### Key Concept
> When you beg a child to behave, you are (1) thinking for the child, (2) taking the responsibility for his behavior, and (3) getting caught up in the Little Adult Assumption.

You are trying to finish up an important activity before lunch and you get this question:

"Can I get a drink?"

"Not right now."

"Why not?"

"Because we're going to lunch in five minutes. We'll stop for water then."

Is there anything wrong with this conversation? No. The child asks a clear question, and the teacher gives a clear answer. The problem, however, is that some kids won't leave it there; they will press the issue further by adding, often in a whiny voice, "But I want a drink now."

What are you going to do at this point? You're a little aggravated, and you've already given the necessary explanation. Should you repeat yourself? Try to elaborate on your answer? Ignore the child?

Let's play this situation out in three scenes. Scene I will star a teacher who believes that kids are little adults. Words and reasons will solve everything and change the child's behavior. We'll see what happens with that approach.

In Scene II, our teacher will be getting smarter. She will start the 1-2-3 program, but the child won't be used to it yet.

In Scene III, the teacher will still be using the 1-2-3 program, and her thirsty little pupil will have grown more accustomed to it.

SCENE I: STARRING THE TEACHER WHO BELIEVES KIDS ARE LITTLE ADULTS

"Can I get a drink?"

"Not right now."

"Why not?"

"Because we're going to lunch in five minutes. We'll stop for water then."

"But I want a drink now."

"I just told you to wait five minutes."

"You never let me do anything."

"What!? Of course I do. You've been line leader all week."

"You let José get a drink."

"Do you have to do everything José does? Besides, *he* finished his work."

"I promise I'll do all my work."

"I've heard that before. Look at your folder! It's full of unfinished work."

"I'm going to tell my parents!"

"Fine. Be my guest!"

You can see where trying to talk at the wrong time can get you. Though everything the teacher said was true, her talking only made the situation worse.

In the next scene, the teacher is getting smarter and uses the 1-2-3 program, but it's new and the child is still getting used to it.

SCENE II: STARRING THE TEACHER BEGINNING THE 1-2-3 PROGRAM

"Can I get a drink?"

"Not right now."

"Why not?"

"Because we're going to lunch in five minutes. We'll stop for water then."

"But I want a drink now."

"That's 1."

"You never let me do anything!"

"That's 2."

"I'm going to tell my parents!"

"That's 3, take five."

That went much better. The temporarily unhappy child goes for a time-out and the episode is over.

How's it going to go when the child is more used to counting and realizes that testing and manipulation are useless?

SCENE III: THE 1-2-3 PROGRAM AFTER A FEW DAYS

"Can I get a drink?"

"Not right now."

"Why not?"

"Because we're going to lunch in five minutes. We'll stop for water then."

"But I want a drink now."

"That's 1."

(Pause.) "Oh, all right." (Grumpy stomping back to desk.)

Good work by the teacher again. She doesn't have to count the grumpy "Oh, all right" because the comment isn't so bad, and the child is getting back to work. If the child had said, "Oh, all right, you stupid jerk!", that would be an automatic 3 and a larger consequence.

Is ignoring the child's badgering an option? In a situation like this, ignoring is more an option for parents at home than for teachers in the classroom. Why? Because badgering and whining disrupt class. In general—and especially in the beginning—counting is best for teachers.

The Benefits of Counting

There are a lot of benefits to using the 1-2-3 program to manage difficult childhood behavior. Here are just a few of them.

Energy Savings!

The 1-2-3 method will save you a lot of breath—and a lot of aggravation. Teachers and parents say counting makes discipline a whole lot less exhausting. Give one explanation, if absolutely necessary, and then you count. There is no extra talking and no extra emotion. You stay calmer and you feel better—about the children and about yourself—when you get a good response at 1 or 2.

When is an explanation or more talking absolutely necessary? In those instances when the problem involved is something that the child does not understand, when his behavior was unusual or fairly serious, or when you really need more information from him about what happened. Examples might include the use of bad language, mocking another student's behavior, or leaving one's area at an inappropriate time.

> **Quick Tip**
>
> One explanation—if really necessary—and then you count. You'll save a lot of breath and a lot of aggravation. When you stay calm, you feel better about your students and about yourself as a teacher.

More Time for Work and Fun

It's sad to say, but in many situations, careless attempts at discipline take up lots of time. The Talk-Persuade-Argue-Yell-Hit syndrome can run its course in less than a minute, but it can also ruin twenty minutes of class time. Everyone is agitated and angry. The teacher does not enjoy being around her students, and the kids do not like being around their teacher.

With the 1-2-3 method, the issue is usually settled in a matter of seconds. Are the children frustrated when they are counted and don't get their way? Of course, but they get over it more quickly than they would if you and they just spent half an hour or so trying to persuade, argue, and yell each other into submission. After counting, things quickly go back to normal, and everyone can continue working. You can enjoy the kids, and they can enjoy you. There is not only more time to get the work done, but you also have the energy you need to get through the day.

Your Authority Is Not Negotiable

You would go crazy if every day you had to negotiate issues like allowing drinks of water, lining up, transitioning, getting work done, and whining. But you shouldn't have to, because you are the boss. As a matter of fact, as a teacher, you must frustrate your pupils on a regular basis because you can't possibly give them everything they want.

Many teachers, though, complicate their job of discipline by setting two goals for themselves instead of just one. The first goal is to discipline the children, which is fine. But the second goal is *to get the kids to like it!* Like the teacher in Scene I of the Drink of Water example, the teacher talks and talks and talks, waiting for the youngster to say something like, "Gee, I never looked at it like that before. Thanks for taking the time to explain it to me. I appreciate your efforts to teach me to be a responsible child."

Let's get real. There's the Little Adult Assumption lurking in the back of your brain again. If your student does listen all the time and more talking seems to help, fine. But with frustrated children, that is not usually the case; too often all that talking escalates to arguing and worse.

The Punishment Is Short and Sweet

1-2-3 Magic is a control on the kids, but it's also a control on the adults. As a teacher, it's not always easy to be reasonable, especially when you're angry. We knew of a fifth-grade teacher once who would use this tactic when one of her students was acting up: "Anyone who thinks that Bryan is acting like a kindergartner, raise your hand." This is an example of an unusual and rather cruel punishment.

Some teachers (especially authoritarian ones) are vulnerable to episodes of yelling, name-calling, or belittling. But with 1-2-3 Magic, the consequences are reasonable, well-defined, and just potent enough to do the job: a time-out might last approximately one minute per year of the child's life or even less.

This brief and reasonable consequence does not make the child so mad that he wants to wage a war of retaliation. With the counting regimen, for example, most kids come back from time-out having forgotten about the whole thing. And the adult's not being allowed to bring up and rehash what happened—unless absolutely necessary—also helps the situation quickly return to normal.

Easy for Others to Learn

The 1-2-3 program is also easy enough to learn so you can train other staff members to use it. Parents who are using 1-2-3 Magic at home often tell their child's teachers about the program. In turn, teachers who use 1-2-3 Magic in class often share the idea with parents who are struggling with their child's behavior at home.

When kids get the same message from everyone at home and at school, this cross-situation consistency makes the program more powerful and easier for the children to learn. "That's 1" at home—and school—means "You're doing something wrong, and it's time to shape up."

We have found that home/school coordination of the 1-2-3 program is especially helpful with children who exhibit particularly difficult behavior. When both parents and teachers use counting fairly and consistently, and when they also respect the No Talking and No Emotion rules, we have seen positive transformations take place for some kids with very challenging behavior.

Time-Out Alternatives (TOAs)

For various reasons, there may be times when you do not want to use a time-out as the consequence for a child's arriving at a count of 3. Perhaps there isn't an opportunity for a time-out when you're dashing out the door to music class, perhaps you feel you want a consequence with a little more clout, or perhaps you want a consequence that fits the "crime." The judicious use of time-out alternatives can be of great value.

Here are some TOA possibilities:

- Loss of privilege
- Small chore or assignment
- Larger chore or assignment
- Note home or call home
- Visit to principal
- Reduced computer time

- Missed opportunity to earn sticker
- Detention
- Reduced preferred activity (free) time

Fines, chores, and losses like these can be very useful as consequences, and there are probably many other options. The list of timeout alternatives is limited only by your imagination. Remember to keep the punishments fair and reasonable; your goal is to teach the child to behave better next time, not to be cruel or get revenge.

Consequences can also be what some people call logical or natural, which means the punishment fits the misbehavior. Consequences can also be tailored to a particular situation. A count of 3, for example, might mean missing the end of an entertaining assembly. Remember when applying natural consequences that kids are still just kids. Exasperated lectures from you along the lines of "Well, this wouldn't have happened if you'd simply listened to me in the first place" are unnecessary. Needless conversation from you also interferes with the child's ability to appreciate the connection between his behavior and its consequences.

CHAPTER SUMMARY
The Benefits of Counting

1. Energy savings
2. More time for work and fun
3. Authority not negotiable
4. Punishment short and sweet
5. Easy for others to learn

7

ADVICE FOR NEARLY ANY COUNTING CHALLENGE

Answers to Our Most Frequently Asked Questions

THE 1-2-3 COUNTING STRATEGY is straightforward, but managing kids' irritating behavior is never an easy job. At this point, you probably have a few questions about this first big phase of the 1-2-3 program. Let's take a look at some of the most important and frequently asked ones.

How long do you take between counts?

First of all, after giving a student a count of 1 (or 2), remember that it is important to continue what you were doing before the misbehavior began. If you were teaching a lesson, keep teaching. It's even more important to focus on and praise the students who are doing well.

With that in mind, you can take as little as five seconds between counts. This brief period is just long enough to allow the child time to shape up. Remember that we're counting Stop (undesirable) behavior, such as arguing, whining, talking, and teasing. For obnoxious behavior like this, it takes a child only one second to cooperate with you by stopping the annoying activity. We certainly don't want to give a child ten minutes to continue misbehaving before giving him a 2 or 3.

Counting is designed to produce the one second's worth of motivation necessary for cooperation. We give the kids five seconds, though, which is a little more generous. Why five seconds? Because this brief pause gives children time to think things over and then do the right thing. In those few seconds—provided the adult keeps quiet about the misbehavior and continues the classroom activity—kids learn to take responsibility for their own behavior.

If a child reaches a 1 or a 2, does he stay at that count for the rest of the day, even if he does nothing else wrong?

No. The time perspective of children is shorter the younger they are. You would not say "That's 1" at 9:00 in the morning, "That's 2" at 11:15, and "That's 3, take five" at 3:00 in the afternoon to a five-year-old. So we have what we call our "window of opportunity" rule: you will have a predetermined period of time during which children can get counted up to 3. For children younger than first graders, for example, the window can be as short as fifteen to thirty minutes, and it can also be somewhat flexible. For first grade through fifth, the windows should be broken up by academic subject and natural transitions (reading, math, lining up for lunch, and so on). For departmentalized schedules in middle school, the window, of course, must be the entire class period of forty-five or fifty minutes. You can adapt these timelines for your own use.

A four-year-old preschooler, for example, might get 3 counts within twenty minutes and consequently earn a time-out. If this same four-year-old, however, got a count of 1, then thirty minutes went by before the child misbehaved again, the supervising adult might go back to the count of 1.

Very few small children manipulate this rule by doing one thing, allowing thirty minutes to pass, and then figuring, "Now I get a free one!" If you feel a child is trying to get away with this, simply make the next count a 2 instead of going back to 1.

The window of opportunity should generally be longer as kids get older, but there are no hard and fast guidelines. Classroom teachers in the primary grades do not usually use a short window because, with twenty-five children in the class, this would allow for too much potential misbehavior in too short a period of time. Some teachers "start over" (all counts are erased) at the end of each academic period. For most first- through fifth-grade teachers, though, the counting period in school is expanded to cover the entire morning, all counts are washed away at lunchtime, and the afternoon is treated as a new and separate window. Most youngsters like the "lunchtime amnesty," which also helps motivate them to behave better in the afternoon.

How do I set up my time-out area? Does the time-out area have to be a sterile, boring environment?

The time-out area should be a place that is clearly separated from the group. It is best to have minimal distractions there. While some children benefit from having clay or drawing paper to help them "process" their feelings, you certainly don't want to create a "fun" environment for the students because then they may misbehave on purpose. Remember, the goal is for the pupil to be separated for a short period to reflect on his or her behavior and then rejoin the group.

Some teachers use a specific chair or a rug for a time-out, while others use a regular desk or table so a child can do schoolwork. We usually prefer that visual contact between the child serving time-out and the rest of the class be broken or limited during the time-out period, so the child can't bother others or be bothered by them.

Teachers are often very creative in coming up with places for time-outs. After prearranging this with a colleague, a number of teachers have had a child who hits 3 actually serve the time-out in a neighboring classroom. The child simply uses a hall pass to walk to the other room, sits in a predetermined spot for five minutes or so, and then returns. (Make sure to check your school's policy for kids walking in the halls.) With kids who may be more unruly, time-outs may be served in a similar fashion in the waiting area of the principal or assistant principal's office. In these situations, no one should carry on a conversation with the student ("How's your day going?") or even kid around with them ("Oh no, not again!"). Support staff should simply observe the child and make sure he or she returns to class at the appropriate time.

Some teachers worry that the time-out itself is not acting as an effective deterrent for misbehavior. This can sometimes happen, but if you really feel time-out is not effective, consider three things first. To begin with, are you still talking too much and getting too emotional during discipline efforts? Adult outbursts ruin everything. Second, if you feel you are remaining calm and time-out is still not working, consider changing the time-out place. Perhaps the principal's waiting area would work better than your classroom. Third, consider time-out alternatives if you believe they may be more effective.

Can you count different misbehaviors to get to 3?

Yes. You don't have to have different counts for each different kind of misbehavior. Imagine this: "Let's see, he's on a 2 for teasing his classmate. He's on a 1 for chewing gum. He's on a 2 for whining at me. He's on a 1 for being out of his seat..."

This routine would soon drive you insane, and you'd need a personal computer to keep track of everything. So for example, if the child teases a classmate, "That's 1"; makes a rude comment, "That's

2"; and then whines at you for counting him, "That's 3, take five." The child is on his way to time-out.

Quick Tip

Don't forget—you can count different misbehaviors to get to 3. That's a lot easier on your aging memory bank. Also, you can give a 1 and your TA can give the 2. The 1-2-3 program works a lot better if the kids know you're both doing it.

If there is a teacher's aide or assistant in the room, the teacher could say "1," the assistant could say "2," and either adult could say "That's 3." The assistant can also start the counting at 1. In fact, we encourage you to share the joy. Actually, it's better if all adults in the room count because then the kids know that this is a consistent plan. The involvement of multiple adults also makes it easier for the children to shape up. In a similar way, the involvement of both home and school in doing the 1-2-3 also makes it easier for kids to behave—especially children with really difficult behavior.

What if the child won't go to time-out?

This is our most frequently asked question. We have all run into that stubborn little one who says, either with words or body language, "No, I'm not going, and you can't make me!"

Key Concept

"What if the student won't go to time-out?" is the most frequently asked question at 1-2-3 Magic workshops. Fortunately, this problem is manageable if you are prepared for it and if you also know how to avoid a power struggle.

So there you are with twenty-five to thirty other pairs of eyes watching you and thinking, "What will she do?" You must appear to be in control at all times—even without saying a word.

The first bit of advice is this: Don't panic. It's OK! This kind of refusal happens all the time. It does not mean you are a lousy disciplinarian or that your whole class is going to spin out of control. Right at this moment, it is critical that you remember to use the No Talking and No Emotion rules. What you also need to remember is that this difficulty is the student's problem, not yours. He has made a poor choice, and he will have to live with it. You cannot force a child to do something. What you can do, however, is guide him to making better choices.

The Issue of Physical Contact: While parents may be able to escort or even carry a reluctant youngster to the time-out area, teachers are not typically able to physically move students from one place to another. This is a safety issue for the student and for the teacher. When a nonfamily member puts her hands on a child, that child may lash out physically, which runs the risk of escalating the situation. Unless the safety of other students is in jeopardy, therefore, we recommend a hands-off approach. This recommendation also fits with the laws and policies of most school districts. If you are uncertain, check with your administrator.

Another reason to refrain from physical contact is that doing so changes the nature of the teacher-student interaction. If we want the message to be "You need to take responsibility for your own behavior," then we do not want to change that message to "If you don't do what I ask, I will do it for you."

There are two exceptions to this rule. If you have a two- to four-year-old who is used to holding your hand, you may take her to time-out holding her hand. With students in K–3, you may walk beside them with your arm out, guiding them to time-out. The bottom line is that students need to get there quickly and safely with as little assistance from the adult as possible.

If the student continues to refuse to go to time-out, you do have a few options.

Option 1: Do Nothing: Your first option is to do nothing. You have said, "Take five," and the student knows what that means. Walk away and pay attention to someone who is behaving well. You may look back and see that the student has gone to time-out. If that is the case, start the time right away. Some students need to save face, and if you are standing right over them demanding they go to time-out, their oppositional urge becomes greater, giving rise to a full-fledged power struggle. When you walk away, however, the choice is squarely on the shoulders of the student, and he has no one to "fight."

If, in addition, you have stuck to the No Talking and No Emotion rules, this makes it easier for the child to decide to go on his own.

What if you walk away and look back and the kid is still sitting there? Here are some other ideas.

Option 2: Offer a Choice: So you have walked away, focused on other students for a couple of minutes, and given your pupil a chance to make the choice on his own. But he is still sitting at his desk. What next? You go to the student and quietly say, "You have a choice. You can take the time-out at your desk or in the time-out area." If the student is then quiet and calm at his desk for the next five minutes, you can say, "I'm glad you took your time-out at your desk. You may join us now."

It is important that this sequence looks like it was your idea and you meant for it to happen. Later, it will be important to set up a time to talk with the student (see chapter 19). This talk should happen at another time—not when the child is misbehaving and not right after he finishes a time-out. During this separate appointment, you will tell the student that you want him to learn to go to the time-out area and that you would like to set up a plan for doing so. Perhaps this is a time to set up a chart, and when the student goes to time-out right away, he earns a star on the chart (see the eight Start behavior tactics in chapter 13). Some kids need this extrinsic motivation initially, then you can gradually fade it out later.

Option 3: Fine the Student: If you have some kind of token economy in your room in which your students can earn points to put toward privileges, you can give the child a choice: either go to time-out or pay a fine. This is essentially a time-out alternative. If you do not have a token economy system, the student can owe you time. Before the next preferred activity, he will need to pay back the time before he can engage in that activity. This might be another situation that would warrant a separate conference with the student.

At this point, you may be saying to yourself, "This is a lot of effort for one kid!" In a way it is, but if you are following these guidelines as intended, you will actually be spending less time arguing, pleading, and—in general—disrupting your own class. You are also laying the groundwork for this student to take responsibility for his own behavior. And as he is struggling with this issue, you are free to continue teaching and spending time with the kids who are behaving well.

Option 4: Start a Fun Activity: Start something with the class that is fun. Perhaps you have a game that you play to review math facts. Tell the class that the schedule is going to change a bit and you are going to play the math review game for a few minutes. You can say something like, "All students who are following directions will be able to play the game with us." This sends the message to Mr. I'm-Not-Going-And-You-Can't-Make-Me that he is going to miss out on the game if he does not take his time-out. You can remind him—without talking too much—that as soon as his time-out is taken, he can join the game.

This tactic also works if there is an activity already in the schedule that would motivate the student to take his time-out so he could join the group. For instance, if the student reaches a count of 3 at 1:05 and recess is at 1:15, you may want to remind him that recess is coming up and his time-out needs to be taken before he can participate in recess. Before using this approach, check with your administrator about the school's policy regarding children missing recess.

What if it's 1:15 and the student hasn't taken his time-out? One option is to have the student sit out of recess for the first five minutes. If you have a co-teacher or an assistant, this person can stay with the student for five minutes in the classroom and then bring the child outside. Sometimes the change of venue works to your advantage. If you think, however, that taking the child outside is going to present more problems (e.g., running away), you may need to do an office referral for this student. Office referrals should be discussed with your administrator ahead of time.

What do you do if the child counts you back?

Your seven-year-old pupil is whining at you because you confiscated the toy she was playing with at her desk. You look at her, hold up one finger, and say, "That's 1." She looks back at you, holds up one tiny finger, and says, "That's 1 to you, too!"

What should you do? Oddly enough, this common occurrence sometimes throws even the most confident adults for a loop. They are at a loss how to handle the unexpected rebellion.

The answer is very straightforward. Your pupils do not have the authority to count anyone. The comment means nothing, but it is disrespectful. Therefore, you simply count it by simply holding up two fingers and saying nothing. If the child again mocks your response, she will have just arrived at 3.

What if there is an obvious problem between two or more children, but you didn't see what happened?

Maria comes running up to you and yells, "Bobby should get a 1!" You haven't the slightest idea what the problem is. How should you respond? In general, our rule is this: if you didn't see or hear the argument or conflict, you don't count it.

For example, if you're at the board with your back turned and you hear a ruckus starting between two kids, there's nothing to stop you from saying, "Hey guys, that's 1 for both of you." Of course, you want to use this rule with flexibility. If you feel one child is consistently being victimized by another, you may have to intervene and count just the aggressive child. On the other hand, when tattling seems to be getting out of hand, many teachers decide to count the tattler as well as the original offender.

One of my little preschoolers has a fit every morning when his parent drops him off at preschool. No matter how much the parent tries to reassure him, he continues to scream.

Though separation anxiety is normal in little children, a kid's desperate screams when left at preschool can be very upsetting. Encourage the parent to become the Master of the Quick Exit. When dropping the child off, the parent should kiss the child goodbye, tell the youngster when she'll see him again, and then get out of there! The longer moms and dads stay and the more they talk, the worse they make the scenario. When the Quick Exit routine is applied consistently for a few weeks, most little children will calm down when it's time to say goodbye.

Can you ever ignore an instance of bad behavior?

Yes, but don't ignore much when you're first implementing the 1-2-3 program. In the beginning, when in doubt, count! After a while, when you're getting a good response at 1 or 2, you may be able to let up a little. Let's say, after a few weeks of getting used to the 1-2-3 program, your student does something right in front of you that would normally be counted. Instead of counting right away, just watch the youngster. The child can almost "feel" the count coming. Sometimes, if you say nothing, the child will spontaneously exercise self-control and stop the misbehavior. This response is ideal because now the child is internalizing the rules and controlling himself without direct intervention.

How do you know when you should count? It's not too difficult to tell. Most of the time, if you're irritated about something that is a Stop behavior, you should be counting. Just to be sure, you can also write yourself a list of countable behaviors and then show it to your students. Some teachers have the children help make up the list. You also want to teach the kids appropriate replacement behaviors; instead of whining, for example, suggest the child use a calm, big-girl voice to let you know she's unhappy about something.

The question of ignoring certain types of behavior leaves room for some variation. Why? Because some teachers simply have longer fuses than others. Some teachers, for example, will ignore kids rolling their eyes, stomping off, grumbling, and whining, while others will count. Some teachers will ignore a child's yelling or even pounding walls, as long as he's on his way to time-out. Other adults will lengthen the time-out period for that kind of behavior. Either

Key Concept

How do you know when you should count? Most of the time, if you're irritated about something that is a Stop behavior, you should be counting.

strategy is correct if it is done consistently. You have to clearly define what kinds of child behavior, in your well-considered opinion, are too obnoxious, too rude, too aggressive, or too dangerous. Then make up your mind that those behaviors are the ones that will be counted.

What if you have other people observing or you are doing an activity with another class?

By this time, you can probably anticipate the answer to this question. You will need to (1) get used to counting in front of other people and (2) not alter your strategy one bit when others are watching.

From time to time, other people will be in your classroom when your kids decide to act up. In fact, the presence of other people seems to trigger disruptive behavior in some kids, presenting educators with a complicated challenge: disciplining children while on stage. Among the groups of people who decide to put you in this awkward position are visiting students, other teachers and colleagues, parents, and administrators. Let's examine the problems presented by each group.

Caution

Make sure you don't alter your counting strategy one bit just because other people are watching. Your students can tell if you are worried about the threat of public embarrassment. So get used to doing the 1-2-3 program in front of other people.

Visiting Students: If there are visiting students, count your boys and girls just as you would if no one else were there. If a student gets timed out, he goes to the time-out area. You might explain to the visiting children that you're using the 1-2-3 Magic system and tell them briefly how it works. If a student says to you, "It's so embarrassing when you count me in front of other people," you can respond, "If you don't want to be embarrassed, you can behave."

Another thing you can do in this situation is count the visiting children if they misbehave. After all, it's your classroom. If the visitors' teacher is there, though, you might want to discuss counting ahead of time with the other adult. Many teachers prefer to discipline their own students.

Teachers, Parents, and Administrators: If you have other adults in your room, you may feel more nervous about counting your students. This discomfort is normal. Although you may feel a little self-conscious at first, you'll soon get used to doing the 1-2-3 program under these circumstances. So count! If you don't take the plunge, your pupils will sense that you are much easier to prey on when other people are in your room.

On the other hand, when you count in front of another adult, something surprising may happen that you will enjoy. You're talking to a colleague and one child rudely and loudly interrupts you, demanding a drink of water. You calmly say, "That's 1." Your child not only quiets down, she also goes back to work. The other adult looks at you like, "What did you do?!" Just tell her about 1-2-3 Magic and explain how it works.

What if the child won't stay in time-out?

Most kids will stay in the area for the time-out. Others, however, will come out before their time is up. One option is to start the time-out over if the child comes out prematurely. Some teachers then increase or even double the time of the second rest period. Explain the deal once and then start.

Another option takes us back to the question about a child's refusing to go to time-out. You can offer the child the option of serving the time-out by staying put or having to accept another—and probably worse—consequence. The stronger consequence can be taken from our list of time-out alternatives. The TOA might be the loss of a privilege, a fine, a chore, reduced preferred activity time, detention, or a call home. Keep in mind that the administration of any of these punishments must be done efficiently—with a minimum of adult talking.

Because a problem like not staying in time-out is aggravating, it's easy to forget that this issue can also be addressed as a Start behavior problem. As you'll soon see, more positive tactics such as charting and praise can also help you train your restless student to stay put. For some kids, the possibility of a reward vs. the possibility of a negative consequence can be a potent influence on their behavior.

My kids act up when I am talking to another adult in the classroom. How should I handle this?

Why does it seem that children always act up more when someone else is around? Perhaps the kids are jealous because their teacher is talking to another adult and ignoring them. Perhaps, as well, the youngsters think you are more helpless and less likely to count because you are involved in a separate conversation.

What you do is count the children just as you would in any other situation. You may have to interrupt your conversation to count. That's fine. Another tactic that can be effective is the use of a nonverbal cue. Simply hold up the required number of fingers for the count while continuing your conversation. Some teachers in this situation will count the whole class. At 3, everyone will be required to put their heads down on their desks for five minutes.

Does being counted hurt a child's self-esteem?

Once 1-2-3 Magic is rolling, most kids aren't counted very often. The mere quantity of counts is usually not a problem. Most children will not get any counts for days at a time. On an average day in a regular classroom with twenty-five children, fewer than five children will get any count at all.

For those children who do get counted more often, if you are doing the 1-2-3 program correctly, there should be no significant threat of hurting self-esteem. What will hurt youngsters' self-esteem is all the yelling, arguing, or sarcasm you may use if you don't control yourself and do the program right. In addition, as you will see later, your overall feedback to your boys and girls should be much more positive than negative. And one count is one bit of negative feedback. Therefore, you will want to more than balance your occasional counting with other activities or strategies, such as affection, fun, sympathetic listening, and praise.

Why three counts? Children should respond the first time you ask! Why give the kids three chances to misbehave?

It's interesting to hear different reactions to 1-2-3 Magic. Some people think counting is too dictatorial, while others see counting as a sign of weakness, believing that children shouldn't get three chances to misbehave before being punished.

The reason for three counts is simple: you want to give the kids two chances—the first two counts—to shape up (unless what they did was so serious that it merited an automatic 3). How are children going to learn to do the right thing if they never get a chance? And with counting, the "chance" comes right away—in the first few seconds following the count. That immediate opportunity helps them learn. They're just kids!

> **Quick Tip**
>
> Some people think counting is too dictatorial, while others see counting as a sign of weakness. In reality, counting gives kids a chance to improve their behavior!

Shouldn't the kids apologize?

This is a tough question. If you're currently asking students to apologize for certain misbehavior and that routine is working well, that's fine. Keep in mind, however, that many apologies are really exercises in hypocrisy. Requiring an apology is often simply part of the child's punishment—not a learning experience involving real sorrow or compassion.

For example, imagine a boy and a girl have gotten into a fight. You break up the tussle, then demand that they apologize to one another. The boy glares at the girl, and with a sneer on his face says, "I'm sorry." His tone is forced, begrudging, and sarcastic. Was this a real apology? Of course not. His comment was merely a continuation of the original battle, but on a verbal level. Second, was his statement a lie? The answer is yes. If you want to insist on apologies, make sure that you are not simply asking the children to lie.

Can you ever count the whole class?

Yes! There are those days in a teacher's life when everybody seems to be going nuts at the same time. Everyone is more energetic, for example, during the days right before a vacation or near the end of the school year. And then there are some classes that are just more difficult in the first place.

At times, therefore, it may be helpful to count the entire class. The teacher says, "Class, that's 1 for everyone," or "If this doesn't stop, I'm going to have to count the whole class." After giving a count, of course, the teacher says nothing and stands quietly watching the class. What if the class hits 3? There's not enough room in the time-out area for twenty-five bodies, so one alternative is to simply have the children put their heads down on their desks for five minutes. This helps calm them down anyway. The teacher states when the time-out is up, and the class will continue with its discussion or activity.

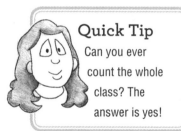

Quick Tip

Can you ever count the whole class? The answer is yes!

Counting the entire class can be tied to a class reward if necessary. For example, the third time in any one month that the whole class is timed out cancels the treat, such as the pizza party.

Two problems with counting the whole class should be kept in mind. First of all, many teachers use this tactic only as a last resort, since it sometimes makes everyone feel bad. Second, inevitably there are children who are not really misbehaving who will get counted along with the class; they may feel this procedure is unfair, but class time-outs are not usually counted on an individual student's record.

Have we taken care of all possible questions? Probably not, but we hope we've covered the most important ones. Now let's take a quick look at several problems that require some minor modifications to the 1–2–3 procedure.

8

HOW TO HANDLE PEER CONFLICTS, POUTING, AND TANTRUMS

Managing Three Common Behavioral Problems

BECAUSE OF THEIR UNIQUE natures, three common, but aggravating, childhood problems require a few minor modifications in our counting procedure. These problems are peer conflicts, temper tantrums, and pouting.

Peer Conflicts

Your life gets exponentially more complicated when you have more than one child acting up. As opposed to a problem with just one child, here there are more actors in the drama, and you may not know exactly what happened to precipitate the fracas. How are you going to handle the situation? There is no need to make things more complex than necessary. Here are two simple and important guidelines that you should follow.

Guideline 1: Count Both Kids

When the children are fighting, most of the time you should count both kids because usually they both helped produce the conflict. Keep in mind that kids are tricky; some provoke in subtle ways and others in more aggressive ways. So it is often hard to tell who started a fight—even if you are right there.

How many times have you been out at recess and, all of a sudden, you hear two children arguing? Count both children unless one is the obvious, unprovoked aggressor and you're absolutely positive about that.

There are times when one child is the obvious, unprovoked aggressor, and these times involve the issue of bullying. Bullies should be supervised closely and counted consistently. If their behavior still does not change, use of the Major/Minor System and one-on-one sessions. Parent conferences will also be necessary.

Guideline 2: Never Ask the World's Two Most Ridiculous Questions

Every adult knows what these questions are: "What happened?" and "Who started it?" What do you expect to get, a version of George Washington's "I cannot tell a lie"? "Yes, I started this fight, and the last thirteen consecutive squabbles have also been my personal responsibility." That kind of confession won't happen. Instead, all you get is the kids blaming one another and yelling.

There are, of course, times when you might need to ask what happened. If, for instance, you think someone might be physically injured, you would want to examine the child and find out what caused the injury.

> **Caution**
>
> Never ask the world's two most ridiculous questions— "Who started it?" and "What happened?"—unless you think a student is physically injured. Do you expect your students to come up with their version of George Washington's "I cannot tell a lie"?

The same thing might be true with other serious or unusual cases. In these situations, ask each child separately for his or her version of the incident. But for your run-of-the-mill issue, trying to find out what happened is too often a lost cause.

Don't expect an older child to act more mature during a fight than a younger child. Even if the two kids involved are eleven years old and six years old, don't say to the eleven-year-old, "She's only a first grader; can't you put up with a little teasing?" The younger child will be sure to both appreciate your generosity and also to take maximum advantage of it.

Key Concept

Don't expect an older child to act more mature during a fight than a younger child.

What if the kids have a fight in the classroom and they both need to go to the time-out area? It would not be a good idea to send two fighting children to the same time-out place to continue their argument. Send them to two separate places or use time-out alternatives. On the playground or at lunch, however, both kids can take their time-out spaced well apart on either side of you.

Pouting

Pouting is a passive behavior that is designed to make you feel guilty. Try not to feel guilty when a child sulks after receiving consequences for misbehavior. Why should you feel bad for trying to be an effective teacher, just because the youngster didn't like the request or restriction you placed on her? You shouldn't.

So if you discipline a child and she gives you the ultimate in martyr looks, just turn around, say nothing, and walk away. The only time you would do something different is if you get what we call an "aggressive pouter." An aggressive pouter is a child who follows you all over the room to make sure you don't miss a minute of her sour face. If she does that, "That's 1." She's trying to rub your nose in her grumpiness, and you're not going to allow her to do that.

Temper Tantrums

Throwing a tantrum is an eminently countable activity, and most kids who throw tantrums will wind up in time-out in less than thirty seconds. As a matter of fact, 1-2-3 Magic has been very effective in eliminating tantrum behavior in many children. That's the good news. The bad news is that a child's tantrum in a classroom presents a problem to a teacher that a home-based tantrum does not present to parents.

Let's say one of your pupils got timed out for throwing a tantrum. He's now in the time-out area, and he's still having a fit. The problem here involves two things: (1) what if the child is disturbing the rest of the class; and (2) what if the time-out period is up but the child is not done with the tantrum? You don't want to let him out in his condition and, in a sense, he's just earned another time-out.

For parents at home, the answer to this dilemma is simple: the time-out doesn't start until the tantrum is over. So if it takes the youngster fifteen minutes to calm down, the time-out starts after fifteen minutes. And if it takes the youngster at home two hours to calm down, the time-out starts in two hours. Under this regime, kids quickly learn that their tantrum is useless and unsatisfying, and they soon cease and desist.

However, what about the classroom situation? Can this same technique be used? The answer to this question requires a judgment call on the part of the teacher that will be based on two things: how much the teacher feels the class is disturbed by the child's fit and how much the teacher herself is disturbed by the child's fit. Older children, for example, are often less bothered by other kids' tantrums (and older children throw fewer tantrums as well). It is also true that teachers vary tremendously with regard to how they perceive children's angry behavior. There are some adults who seem to feel that pouting is the same as throwing a tantrum.

So, our conclusion is this:

1. Do nothing for fifteen to thirty seconds
2. Offer the child a choice of calming or accepting a time-out alternative
3. Make an office referral

If teacher and class tolerance of the child's angry outbursts are not high, use these three steps as they are described above when a child throws a tantrum. If the teacher and class are not particularly bothered by a tantrum, extend the time for step 1. We recommend the use of a kitchen timer that is controlled by the adult. Tell the student, "I will start your time when you are calm and quiet." Then focus on the rest of the class as you praise the kids for ignoring the inappropriate behavior.

One caution: don't be constantly reprimanding the angry student every few minutes by saying things like, "Come on now, don't you think that's enough?" Comments like that simply give the frustrated little one the exquisite satisfaction of knowing that his retaliation is successful. When the student finally does calm down, you say, "I am starting your time," and do so. Instead of using a timer, some teachers say to the child, "You can rejoin the group when you are ready." However, make sure the child is really ready when he wants to return, and say nothing about the incident afterward.

CHAPTER SUMMARY

1. Peer conflicts: count both kids most of the time.
2. Temper tantrums: the time-out might not start until after the tantrum is over.
3. Pouting: can be ignored unless the child becomes an "aggressive pouter."

9

GETTING STARTED
WITH COUNTING

How to Talk to Your Class about 1-2-3 Magic and the New Classroom Rules

IT TAKES ONLY A short period of time to get the students oriented to the 1-2-3 discipline system.

The teacher should explain the program in detail each day during the first week of school. During the second week, class discussions are geared toward the children telling the teacher how the system works. This exercise helps the teacher know how well the class understands the process and which kids may be having trouble. Use your judgment in deciding when to discontinue these discussions.

If you work with an assistant or another teacher, it's preferable if both staff members do the initial explaining to the kids. It is also helpful to have a poster or some sort of visual representation to refer to as you provide this information. The behavior stoplight, which we'll describe on page 67, can work nicely for this purpose. You may also want to refer to the four or five positively stated rules posted in your classroom when you are discussing countable offenses.

It is also important to set high expectations for your students from the beginning. Here is an example of a kickoff conversation at the elementary level. The teacher holds up a "mystery bag" in front of the class and says: "Class, let me have your attention. I need to discuss something new we will be doing, and I need your help. First of all, take a minute to think about what I might have in this bag. When you have a guess, raise your hand."

Quick Tip

It's important to set high expectation for your students from the beginning.

The teacher gives the students some "think time" and then calls on a couple of students for guesses. This is a way to engage the students and capture their attention. After a few guesses have been shared, the teacher reveals that there is a model car in the bag. She says: "Well, I have this model car here for a reason. It is going to be a symbol of what we discuss today. Who can tell me what a driver should do when he comes to a red light?" The teacher calls on a student to answer and then says: "That's right, the driver must stop. That's the rule. What happens if the driver does not stop and a police officer sees him?" The teacher calls on a student to answer and then says: "That's right, the driver gets a ticket or a consequence. So it is important for adults and children to follow rules and laws; if they don't, someone might get hurt.

"We are going to have a new rule in our classroom. The rule is that when you are doing something you shouldn't, you are going to get two chances to shape up. If you don't, you are going to have to take a time-out. So the first time you misbehave, I will say, 'That's 1.' If you keep going, I will say, 'That's 2.' If you continue, I will say, 'That's 3, take five.' Hopefully, you will behave after a count of 1 or 2 and we can forget the whole thing. Let's practice."

Role-Playing

One way to answer a lot of the children's questions about 1-2-3 Magic is to practice the discipline steps by role-playing. It is important to set up the expectations for the role-play before you begin. Here is how it works. The teacher asks the students to think of an inappropriate behavior that breaks the rules but is not unsafe. She lets the students know that she is going to call on a few students to demonstrate.

If there is another adult in the room, it is wise to model the counting process for the students before calling on them. Teacher A pretends he's acting up by whining or yelling. Teacher B firmly counts Teacher A with a 1. Teacher A continues his misbehavior, so he advances to 2 and then 3. Teacher B sends Teacher A to the time-out area. Teacher A cooperates but looks a little grumpy. Your students may giggle. The children won't giggle when you start counting them, but the role-play will help them get the idea.

> **Quick Tip**
>
> Have your students role-play the counting procedure before you actually start. Teacher B may count Teacher A, who pretends to be a child acting up. Then have the kids do some of the role-playing themselves. Some teachers make a point to involve potentially difficult kids in the role-play so these youngsters identify with the program.

When modeling, show a scenario in which the "student" makes it all the way to time-out and a scenario in which the student shapes up after 2 and remains with the group. After the modeling phase, call on two or three students to practice. Some teachers like to start with a relatively compliant child who will model the procedure correctly. Other teachers, however, start with a child who they think might actually be quite troublesome during the coming year and let that child role-play the part of a teacher counting. Then that same child role-plays being counted and timed out. The objective here is to get the student's cooperation and help him identify with the program in its early stages.

Parent Orientation

Parents and guardians can be oriented to 1-2-3 Magic in two ways.

1. On the first day of school, a note may be sent home describing the discipline program and the classroom rules. This note is to be signed and returned. This process helps make sure that the parents understand the system and have agreed to it. The note may also be helpful at a later date if a conference is required about behavioral problems.
2. As part of Back to School Night or parent-teacher conferences, you can explain the discipline procedures to the parents and encourage comments and questions. You can also show the *1-2-3 Magic* book and video as references at parent night; encourage parents to borrow them to familiarize themselves with the program, as the program works even better if it is used both at school and at home.

Starting the 1-2-3 Process

During the first few days of school, you can post four or five important classroom rules, such as "Follow Directions," "Be a Friend," "Listen Carefully," and "Do Your Own Work" on the wall in the classroom. During the first two weeks, you should explain what these rules mean and also what will be counted, such as getting out of your seat, not raising your hand, arguing or fighting with someone, pushing in line, talking at the wrong time, and tattling.

You can also count "attitude." This can include excessive expressions (verbal or nonverbal) of disrespect, anger, or excessive pouting.

For children this age, getting a time-out is a big deal. Many young children will become teary if they are counted at all, but especially if they are counted to 3. Some of this is simply due to embarrassment, which in moderation is not harmful.

Remember that for the purpose of the 1-2-3 program, the school day for first through fifth graders is usually divided into segments based on school subjects. Warnings can add up to 3 during reading or math, but after the transition to a new subject or activity, everyone returns to 0 and starts fresh.

For the kindergartners and preschoolers, the counting window will be shorter, perhaps fifteen to thirty minutes. And for departmentalized middle school kids, the window is usually one class period.

Counting can also be done in special classes, such as music, art, gym, library, and computer. Those counts are sometimes kept separate from the regular classroom discipline program due to the difficulty involved in communicating this information to the main classroom teacher.

Behavioral Accounting

Teachers have a unique problem that parents don't have: no parent has to discipline twenty-five kids at home. A teacher must keep an eye on the entire class and also keep track of which kids are at which counts.

Quick Tip

Want to keep track of who's on what count? You should have a consistent system. For many teachers, that system is the behavior stoplight.

However, the job is not as daunting as it first appears. In a regular classroom on an average day, most children will not be counted at all. In a class of twenty-five students, it is unusual if more than three or four kids receive a count of any kind, and on many—or even most—days, no one will receive a time-out.

Still, some kind of record keeping is necessary, and several options are available. Some teachers use the old blackboard routine. With the first count, the child's name goes on the board. The second and third counts result in check marks after the name. If the child goes to 3, he or she serves the time-out and their name can be erased. Many teachers feel, however, that writing the offender's name on the board is too much like "rubbing it in." In addition, sometimes the names do not

get erased when they are supposed to, causing unfair embarrassment the next day.

One teacher came up with a more creative idea. She made a big stoplight (approximately 24 inches by 6 inches) out of cardboard, with the usual red light on top, yellow in the middle, and green on the bottom. She laminated it and hung a strip of black vinyl from the bottom. Attached to the vinyl were clothespins, and on each clothespin was the name of a child.

If a child received a count, he had to get up and move his clothespin from the vinyl to the green light, which stood for a count of 1. The same procedure was followed for a count of 2 (clothespin on the yellow light), and finally, if the child hit 3, the clothespin was put on the red light while the time-out was served. Upon leaving the time-out area, the youngster was then allowed to put his name back on the black vinyl strip.

The advantage of this setup is that at any one time you can simply glance at the stoplight and see where every student in the class is. On the other hand, the names are not as large and obvious as they are when written on the board. Other record-keeping setups using big, colored numbers or colored containers (with names on Popsicle sticks) can work equally well.

Despite the ease of these methods, some teachers feel that less notoriety is better with any behavioral accounting procedure, especially when dealing with children in the higher grades. One easy method involves the teacher merely writing the student's name on a small notepad when giving the first count or warning. Further counts are then marked after the name.

Since few kids normally get counted in the first place, some teachers just keep the counts in their heads. This tactic shouldn't be used, though, unless it can be done accurately. Keep in mind that many

> **Quick Tip**
> One easy method of keeping track of counts is to write the student's name on a small notepad when giving out counts or warnings.

children also keep track—both for themselves as well as for their classmates—and they may try to correct a teacher who is at the wrong number. Students also may not think an instructor is serious about counting if the adult does not have an obvious and systematic way of keeping track of the counts.

After your initial explanations of 1-2-3 Magic, don't expect your students to be grateful, to look enlightened, or to thank you for your efforts to teach them responsibly. Just get going, stick to your plan, and—when in doubt—count!

What about two- and three-year-olds who won't understand an initial explanation? Just start counting and doing time-outs. Little kids are much smarter than we often give them credit for being. They'll get the idea quickly.

At this point of the book, you may feel that you're ready to start using the 1-2-3 program. Not so fast! If you began counting right now, you wouldn't be prepared for the fact that some children are going to give you a hard time in the beginning. That may be the bad news, but the good news is that we have discovered and identified the Six Kinds of Testing and Manipulation. Once you understand these tactics and what's behind them, you'll be ready for almost anything.

CHAPTER SUMMARY

Use role-playing, parent involvement, and behavioral accounting to prepare your students for 1-2-3 Magic.

 Almost ready!

PART III

Managing Testing and Manipulation

CHAPTER 10
Recognizing the Six Kinds of Testing and Manipulation

CHAPTER 11
Tales from the Trenches

CHAPTER 12
More Serious Offenses

10

RECOGNIZING THE SIX KINDS OF TESTING AND MANIPULATION

How to Prepare for Kids Resisting 1-2-3 Magic

ONE OF THE UNFORTUNATE parts of being a grown-up is that you cannot give children everything they want. To make matters worse, you must also regularly ask students to start doing things they often don't want to do (schoolwork, cleaning up) and to stop doing some things they often do want to do (talking, whining, running in the hallway). The fact of the matter is that in addition to being warm, caring, and supportive, you must also frustrate your students on a regular basis.

When you are expecting something from your students, the children have two choices. First, they can cooperate and tolerate whatever frustration they might feel. Most kids soon learn that frustration is not the end of the world, and they may even begin to get a sense that putting up with present aggravations may actually be the route to future rewards. The children may also begin to enjoy their schoolwork—at least some of the time. On the other hand, when they feel frustrated, kids can engage in what we call "testing and manipulation." Testing and manipulation are the efforts of the frustrated child to get what he wants or to avoid discipline by getting his teacher confused and, consequently, sidetracked.

Several things need to be remembered about testing and manipulation:

1. **Testing and manipulation occur when a child is frustrated.** For example, you are not giving your pupil the snack he wants; you are counting him; you are making him do work or come in from recess. He doesn't like this and hopes for a way to get what he wants in spite of your efforts.

2. **Testing and manipulation are purposeful behaviors.** The first purpose of a child's testing behavior is obviously to get his way rather than have you impose your will. But testing and manipulation can have another purpose. If the child still cannot get his way, he will try to get something else: revenge. Though it is aggravating at times, this childhood desire to retaliate is perfectly normal.

3. **When engaging in testing and manipulation, a child has a "choice" of six basic tactics.** All six can serve the first purpose of getting one's way; five of the six tactics can serve the second purpose, revenge. Usually a child's testing behavior will represent a combination of one or more of the basic manipulative tactics.

Both teachers and parents will quickly recognize the tactics we are about to describe—you have likely encountered each of them many times with your students.

By the way, the use of testing and manipulation does not necessarily mean that a child is emotionally troubled or in need of psychological care. Attempts by kids to get their way, as well as attempts to "punish" the bigger people who don't give them their way, are normal human psychological tactics. The use of testing also does not require an exceptionally high IQ. In fact, adults are often amazed at how naturally and how skillfully little kids are able to produce and modify complex testing strategies. Because they are so naturally skilled, it is very important that teachers understand children's testing tactics and how to manage them.

The Six Basic Testing Tactics

Here are the six fundamental strategies that children use to attempt to influence the adults who are frustrating them:

> **Key Concept**
> The first goal of testing is for the child to get what he wants. Since he's less powerful than his teacher, he must use some kind of emotional manipulation. The second goal of testing is to get revenge, especially if the first goal is frustrated.

1. Badgering: "Why? Why? Why? Why?"

Badgering is the "Please, please, please, please!" or "Why, why, why?" routine. "Just this once! Just this once! Just this once! Just this once!" There are some children who could have been machine guns during the last World War. The child just keeps after you and after you and after you, trying to wear you down with repetition. "Just give me what I want and I'll be quiet!" is the underlying message.

Badgering can be particularly taxing when it is done very loudly and also when it is done with other people around, such as the rest of the class! Some teachers attempt to respond to everything a frustrated child says every time she says it. They may try to explain, to reassure, or to distract. As the badgering continues, these teachers can become more and more desperate, going on the equivalent of a verbal wild-goose chase while searching for the right words or reasons to make the child keep quiet. Many kids, however, are extremely single-minded once their badgering starts. They won't stop until they either get what they want or until the adult in charge uses a more effective approach to stop the testing.

Badgering is what we refer to as a great "blender" tactic, since it mixes easily with other manipulative strategies. The basic element in badgering, of course, is repetition. So when any of the other verbal testing tactics are repeated again and again, the resulting manipulative strategy is a combination of that other tactic plus the repetitive power of badgering.

2. Temper (Intimidation): "I Hate You!"

Displays of temper, or what we sometimes refer to as intimidation, are obvious, aggressive behavior. Younger children may throw themselves on the floor, bang their heads, holler at the top of their lungs, and kick around ferociously. Older kids may come up with arguments that accuse you of being unjust, illogical, or simply a bad person in general. When frustrated, some kids may also swear or angrily complain.

Some children's fits of temper go on for very long periods. Many children with ADHD or bipolar disorder, for example, have been known to rant and rave for more than an hour at a time. In the process, they may damage property or break things. Tantrums are often prolonged even further (1) if the child has an audience; (2) if the adult involved continues talking, arguing, or pleading with the youngster; or (3) if the adult doesn't know how to handle the aggression.

Temper fits in two-year-olds can be aggravating, but they can also be funny. As kids get older and more powerful, however, tantrums get more worrisome and scarier. That's why we like to see these fits well-controlled or eliminated by the time a child is five or six.

3. Threat: "I'm Going to Run Home!"

Frustrated kids will sometimes threaten their teachers with dire predictions if the adults don't come across with the desired goods. Here are a few examples:

"I'm going to run home!"
"I'll never speak to you again!"
"I'm going to scream!"
"I'm not eating lunch and I won't do my work!"
"I'm going to tell my parents!"

The message is clear: something bad is going to happen unless you give me what I want immediately. Give me the treat, stop counting me, don't make me work, OR ELSE! Some of the threats that younger children come up with are humorous, while others are not. Some frustrated children threaten to kill themselves, and this is something no one takes lightly. Many adults wonder if the child is just being manipulative or if he or she really wants to die. Most schools have policies in place regarding such comments, so be sure to check with your administrator as to how this situation should be handled.

4. Martyrdom: "I Never Get Anything!"

Martyr-like testing tactics are a perennial favorite of children. When using martyrdom, the child may indicate that his life has become totally unfair and an incredible burden. "No one around here likes me anymore," "I never get anything," or "You like her more than me" are examples.

Or the youngster may actually do something that has a self-punitive, self-denying flavor, such as not eating lunch, sitting in the coat closet for an hour, or staring out the window without talking. Crying, pouting, and simply looking sad or teary can also be effective manipulative devices.

The goal of martyrdom is to make the adult feel guilty, and martyrdom can be surprisingly effective. This testing tactic is very difficult for many adults to handle. Many grown-ups seem to have a "guilt button" the size of the state of Wyoming! All the kids have to do is push that button, and they wind up running the place.

Children learn early on that teachers are highly invested in the welfare of their students. Kids know their caretakers want them to be safe, happy, and healthy. Unfortunately, kids also seem to naturally appreciate the logical consequence of this adult commitment: acting hurt or deprived can be a powerful way of influencing adult behavior.

Two-year-olds, for example, will sometimes hold their breath until they turn blue when they are mad about not getting what they want. Many of us wonder how a little child could even come up with an idea like that. They can and they do!

Caution

When testing and manipulating, the child is making you a deal: you call off your dogs and I'll call off mine. If you then give in and give the student what he wants, the testing will cease immediately. What's the catch? The catch is that you are no longer running your own classroom.

5. Butter Up: "You're the Nicest Teacher in the World!"

The fifth tactic, butter up, takes an approach that's different from the first four. Instead of making you feel uncomfortable, the child tries to make you feel good—at least at the beginning. You may then run the risk of losing this good feeling if you subsequently frustrate the child.

"Gee, Miss Smith, you've got the prettiest eyes of any teacher I know," is a fairly blatant example. Or, "I think I'll go straighten up the bookshelf. It's been looking kind of messy for the last few weeks."

With butter up, the basic message from child to adult is "You'll feel really bad if you mistreat, discipline, or deny me after how nice I've been to you." Butter up is intended to be an advance setup for adult guilt. The child is implying, "You'll feel so positively toward me that you won't have the heart to make me feel bad."

Promises can be used by children as butter-up manipulation. "Please, please. I'll eat my lunch and I promise I won't even have any ice cream," said one little girl who wanted a snack at 9:00 in the morning. Some promises kids make are impossibilities. Have you heard this one? "I'll never ask you for anything ever again."

Apologies can be sincere, but they can also be examples of butter-up testing. "I'm sorry, I'm sorry. I said I'm sorry," one little boy pleaded in an attempt to avoid a trip to the principal's office.

Butter-up manipulation is the least obnoxious of all the testing tactics. In fact, some people don't think it should be labeled as testing at all. It is true that butter up is sometimes hard to distinguish from genuine affection. If a child says, "I like you," and doesn't ask for anything immediately afterward, it's probably genuine affection.

And a child who asks if he can have a sticker if he finishes his work may be proposing a straightforward and legitimate deal. But if you've ever heard a teacher say, "The only time Johnny's nice is when he wants something," that person is probably referring to the butter-up tactic.

6. Physical Tactics: Pow! Whack! Bam!

This form of testing is perhaps the worst. Here the frustrated child may physically attack the adult, break something, or run away. Physical methods of trying to get one's way, of course, are more common in smaller children who don't have well-developed language. When the use of this type of testing continues beyond age four or five, however, we begin to worry. Some kids have a long history of this behavior, and the bigger the child gets, the scarier their physical strategies get.

Other frustrated, physically oriented kids will smash or break things—sometimes even their own possessions. Another physical testing tactic, running away, is not used a lot by younger children, although there have been a few children who have actually left school and run home. Threats to run away—rather than really doing it—appear more often in this age group.

What's Going on Here?

Most kids would never be able to describe the underlying mechanics of testing. But we can tell you exactly what's going on. Four of the tactics we've described—badgering, intimidation, threat, and martyrdom—share a common dynamic. The child, without quite knowing what he's doing, is in effect saying to the teacher something like this: "Look, you're making me uncomfortable by not giving me what I want. But now I'm also making you uncomfortable with my badgering, tantrums, ominous statements, or feeling sorry for myself. Now that we're both uncomfortable, I'll make you a deal: you call off your dogs and I'll call off mine."

Quick Tip
A child who is test-ing you is offering you a deal: give me what I want and my badgering, temper, threat, or martyrdom will stop—immediately! Does that sound like a deal you can't refuse? Think again!

If you do give in and give the child what he wants, you are guaranteed that any testing will stop immediately. In a split second, no more hassles and your classroom will quiet down. Some people say, "Thank heaven. There's a way of getting rid of testing and manipula-tion!" There certainly is, but what's the catch? The catch, of course, is who's running the show? It certainly isn't you; it's the students. All they have to do in a conflict situation is get out their heavy-duty emotional weapons and you are chopped liver.

Who's Pushing Your Buttons?

Think of each of your students, one at a time, and ask yourself, "Does this child have a favorite testing tactic? One that he or she uses frequently or all the time?" If your answer is yes, that's bad news. Why? Because that means the ploy works for the child. People don't generally repeat behavior that doesn't work for them.

Caution
Does the child have a fa-vorite testing tactic? If your answer is yes, that means the strategy is working, either by:
1. Getting the child her way or
2. Allowing her to get re-venge on the adult she is testing

Let's recall the two purposes of testing and manipulation. First of all, a testing strategy works when the child successfully gets his way by using that tactic. How do you know if a child is getting his way by testing? It's obvious—you just give it to him! You give him the snack right before lunch, clean up the blocks for him, or reduce his assignment.

The idea that the testing tactic "works" can also refer to the second purpose of test-ing and manipulation: revenge. Children will repeat tactics that provide an effective way of retaliating against the adults who are causing their frustration. How does a child know if she is effectively getting revenge? The answer takes us right back to the No Talking and No Emotion rules. If your student can get you very upset and get you talking too much, she knows she's got you.

Children know they are getting effective revenge when their teachers start saying things like, "How many times do I have to tell you!", "Why can't you just take 'No' for an answer!!", "ARE YOU TRYING TO DRIVE ME NUTS?!?" The angry part of your young pupil will find comments like these satisfying, and the next time this child is upset with you, he will know exactly how to press the revenge button.

Imagine you want some work done, and your student has a tantrum (tactic 2) because he wants to go on the computer. If you don't follow the No Talking and No Emotion rules, your response turns into a *counter* temper tantrum. You get more upset than the child did! Final score: Student 1, Teacher 0. He got satisfaction from the big, angry splash from the larger, "more powerful" adult.

Other kids retaliate by making their teachers feel guilty. Imagine that when asked to go to the end of the line, a fourth-grade girl resorts to martyrdom (tactic 4): "Well, it's obvious that nobody around here likes me anymore. I might as well transfer to another school" (she adds a touch of threat, tactic 3). You feel frightened and guilty. You are certain that she will have diminished self-esteem. When you get to your destination, you sit the girl down and tell her how much you enjoy having her in your class. You have just been had by tactic 4, martyrdom. You are squirming and uncomfortable, and the child is making you pay for your mistake.

Always remember this: unless you are a grossly neglectful or abusive teacher, your kids know that you like them. And by all means, tell them that you like them, but don't do this when they're pulling a tactic 4 on you. It is also OK to remind the kids that you like them but sometimes you don't like their behavior. This sends the message that the behavior is separate from the child as a person.

How to Manage Testing and Manipulation

Now let's say you're getting into the spirit of 1-2-3 Magic. Your eleven-year-old student wants to call his mom and ask her to bring the homework that he forgot. You deny his request and tell him it's not allowed. The following scene occurs:

"Why not? Come on, just this once!" (badgering)

"Can't do it."

"I never get anything." (martyrdom, badgering)

"I don't think that's the case."

"I'll do double homework tonight." (butter up, badgering)

"That's not an option."

"This stinks—I HATE YOUR GUTS!" (intimidation, badgering)

"Sorry."

The child throws a book on the floor. (physical tactic)

"Stop and think about your choices."

"Please, PLEASE! Oh, come on, my mom won't mind."(badgering)

"I am afraid not."

"If you don't let me, you'll be sorry!" (threat, badgering)

This interaction may be aggravating, but in a way, it's good! Why? Because something constructive is happening. The child is fishing around, switching tactics, and probing for your weak spot. But he can't find a weak spot. You are sticking to the program. Not only that, you are remaining fairly calm in spite of the aggravation.

There is one thing wrong with this example, however, and that has to do with how you handle testing and manipulation. You would not let the child switch tactics that many times (and you would also not talk so much). What should you do? Well, if you look at our list of six testing tactics, five of them (except butter up) are Stop behavior. Stop behavior should be counted. So if a child were pushing you this much, he should be counted.

This is how the scene above should be handled if you were using the 1-2-3 program. Remember that the boy has already been given an explanation:

"Why not? Come on, just this once!" (badgering)

"That's 1."

"I never get anything." (martyrdom, badgering)

"That's 2."

"I'll do double homework tonight." (butter up, badgering)

"That's 3, take five."

The third count is more for the badgering than the butter up, but it's obvious this kid is not going to give up until you gently but firmly put your foot down. That goal is achieved by counting and the resulting time-out.

Remember, with the exceptions of butter up and passive pouting, testing and manipulation should be counted, especially in the beginning, when you're just starting 1-2-3 Magic. Once the kids are used to the discipline system, the less aggressive, less obnoxious forms of testing can—at your discretion—occasionally be ignored. The effectiveness of not responding at all (verbally or nonverbally) to a child's testing can be evaluated by how quickly the child gives up the battle. Many kids will quickly learn that no response at all from you (ignoring) means that this time they are not going to get their way or get effective revenge.

Which Testing Tactic Is the Most Common?

Badgering, temper, threat, martyrdom, butter up, and physical tactics—these are the methods children use to get their way from adults. And all these tactics, except butter up, can also be used by kids to punish the uncooperative adults who obstinately persist in refusing to give the youngsters what they want.

Which strategies are the favorites of your boys and girls? We have taken several surveys of teachers and parents, asking which tactics they thought children used the most. Interestingly, both groups of grown-ups always mention the same three: badgering, temper, and—the overwhelming favorite—martyrdom.

You will also be interested to know that the most annoying manipulative maneuver used by children is a tactic that combines two of the three favorites listed. This tactic, which drives many grown-ups absolutely nuts, is a combination of badgering and martyrdom. The word describing the behavior starts with the letter *w*. You guessed it: whining!

What to Expect in the Beginning

As we mentioned before, once you start counting, the kids will fall primarily into two categories: immediate cooperators and immediate testers. If you're lucky enough to have immediate cooperators, enjoy it! You will feel more effective because the boys and girls are listening to you. You will want to have more fun with your kids, talk with them, praise them, and listen to them. You will enjoy working on building a good relationship. This good relationship, in turn, will make counting (1) less necessary and (2) a lot easier when it is necessary.

Immediate testers, however, show worse behavior at first. When you let them know you're going to be the boss and you take away the power of their favorite testing strategies, the behaviors of these children deteriorate in two ways. Some will *up the ante* with a particular testing tactic. The volume and length of a child's tantrums, for example, may double. Badgering may become more intense or aggressive, and martyrdom may become more whiney and pathetic.

The other unpleasant change you may initially see in noncooperators is *tactic switching*. The kids may try new manipulative strategies you've not seen before, or they may return to others they haven't used for a while. The most common switches involve going from badgering and martyrdom (and whining) to temper. Some kids, quite understandably, blow up when their attempts to wear you down with repetition or make you feel guilty fail. Although tactic switching is aggravating, remember that switching is almost always a sign that you are doing well at sticking to your guns. Keep up the good work!

What do you do when you're faced with tactic escalation and tactic switching? Several things are important to remember:

1. Don't get discouraged; this is a normal stage many children go through while adjusting to 1-2-3 Magic.
2. When necessary, count fairly but aggressively.
3. Keep your mouth shut except for necessary explanations and the counting itself.

Eventually, tactic escalation and tactic switching will diminish, and your students will accept your discipline without having a major fit every time you have to frustrate them. You then have won the battle, and you can spend more time teaching. You are the teacher, they are the children, and your classroom is a more peaceful place.

One final word: some kids, after cooperating initially, become "delayed testers." Delayed testing can occur after the novelty of the new system wears off, when the children begin to realize that they aren't getting their way anymore, or after a time when your daily routine has gotten disrupted.

Quick Tip

When in doubt, count!

If you're unprepared for it, delayed testing can be a bit disillusioning. You think to yourself, "The kids were behaving so well before!" You may feel like the whole system is falling apart or that it was too good to be true. Fortunately, the remedy is not far away. Read *1-2-3 Magic in the Classroom* again, watch the video, discuss the suggestions with other colleagues, and then get back to basics: follow the No Talking and No Emotion rules, be gentle but assertive, and when in doubt, count.

CHAPTER SUMMARY

The Six Kinds of Testing and Manipulation

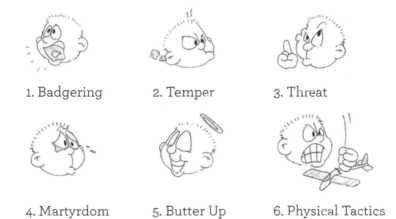

1. Badgering   2. Temper   3. Threat

4. Martyrdom   5. Butter Up   6. Physical Tactics

11

TALES FROM THE TRENCHES

A Glimpse Inside Classrooms Using 1-2-3 Magic

NOW LET'S STUDY SOME examples of the 1-2-3 program in action to give you a feel for how and when counting can be used. Our stories and commentaries will also illustrate some of the basic do's and don'ts involved with the procedure. When the educators in our examples don't do so well with their discipline the first time around, sometimes we'll give them another chance to correct their mistakes.

Peer Relations I

Round One

It's raining outside, so Mrs. Kay's class is having indoor recess. Nine-year-olds John and Brittany are the best of friends and the worst of enemies. They are playing with Legos on the floor. So far Mrs. Kay is amazed the kids are getting along so well, but the fun is about to end.

"Brittany, I need another wheel for my tank," says John.

"No, John, I've got it on my wagon," Brittany says.

(Mrs. Kay squirms in her chair, predicting what will come next.)

"Lemme just use one wheel now. I'll give it back to you later," suggests John.

"No, my wagon needs four wheels," replies Brittany.

"Your wagon looks stupid!"

"Mrs. Kay, John's gonna take one of my wheels and I had them first!"

(Mrs. Kay is not pleased with this tattling.)

"Both of you, settle down!"

"She doesn't need to hog all the wheels. There aren't enough for me to make what I want."

"But I made this first!"

"OK, kids, that's 1 for both of you."

"She's an idiot." *(John smashes his creation and leaves.)*

How Did She Do?

This is a pretty good discipline job by Mrs. Kay. Perhaps she should have counted a little bit sooner instead of growling, "Settle down!" Should she have counted John for smashing his tank or badmouthing his peer? Some teachers would count these behaviors, but others wouldn't because the tank was John's (and it can be rebuilt). John may also be doing the right thing by leaving the situation.

Round Two

Let's give Mrs. Kay another chance to improve her technique:

"Brittany, I need another wheel for my tank," says John.

"No, John, I've got it on my wagon," Brittany says.

(Mrs. Kay squirms in her chair, predicting what will come next.)

"Lemme just use one wheel now. I'll give it back to you later," suggests John.

"No, my wagon needs four wheels," replies Brittany.

"Your wagon looks stupid!"

"Kids, that's 1 for both of you."

(Mrs. Kay is a little irritated.)

"She doesn't need to hog all the wheels. There aren't enough for me to make what I want."

"But I made this first!"

"OK, kids, that's 2."

How Did She Do?

Mrs. Kay did much better this time, especially since she was aggravated. Excellent self-control and an excellent job of not taking out her frustration on the kids. Some teachers would count only John in this situation.

Peer Relations II

Sixth-graders Sean and Tammi are getting into it while trying to play Scrabble during free time. The teacher is writing a note to a parent that has to be sent home today.

"It's my turn."

"No it isn't. You lost it 'cause you took so long."

"Give me that. I was going to pick up that one!"

"You scratched me!"

"I did not, you idiot! You started it!"

"You're so dumb it isn't funny."

(The teacher comes over.)

"What's going on here?"

"She's cheating!"

"I am not, you're too slow!"

"Be quiet, both of you! Tell me what happened."

(General yelling and chaos follow the ill-fated inquiry.)

"OK, that's 1 for both of you."

(General yelling and chaos continue.)

"That's 2."

(Sean dumps the Scrabble board over, grabs a bunch of letters, and throws them down.)

"Sean, that's 3, take 10."

How Did He Do?

The teacher recovered pretty well after asking the world's most ridiculous question. He should have started counting earlier.

Assembly Time

Round One

Rita loves to go to assemblies with the class. The reason she loves them is because they frequently involve singing and dancing, and she likes to join in (at the most inopportune time). Rita's teacher, however, does not enjoy taking her student to the assembly as much as Rita enjoys going. The reason the teacher does not like these events is because, sooner or later, Rita stands up and blocks the students behind her by dancing and singing. The other students and teachers become annoyed, but if Rita's teacher asks her to sit down or to leave, Rita throws a fit. The teacher feels her student is running the show, and she is correct. Here's how the scene goes with Rita sitting next to the teacher at the assembly:

(Rita stands up to sing and dance along with the performers.)

"Rita, you need to sit down."

"But this is so much fun…I want to dance with them."

"I just told you to sit down. The other students can't see."

"I can't see if I sit down!"

"Now stop that! That's enough! Come on, you don't want to have to leave, do you?"

"I never get to do anything!" *(Rita starts crying loudly.)*

"OK, OK! Calm down!" *(The teacher pulls Rita into her lap.)* "Rita, you need to be quiet. The other people can't enjoy the show. If you keep getting up, you will have to leave. Do you understand me?"

"Yes."

"And you promise you won't get up to dance?"

"Yes."

"Say, 'I promise.'"

"I promise."

"OK, go sit down."

Rita does fine for six minutes. Then she starts singing and dancing again. Her teacher pretends she doesn't notice, hoping she will stop.

How Did She Do?

This is a classic example of a child intimidating an adult with the threat of public embarrassment. Rita's teacher is intimidated into a desperate attempt at Little Adult reasoning (other people can't enjoy the show) and the elicitation of futile promises.

Round Two

Let's give the teacher another chance to get this one right.

"I'm so excited about the assembly. Will there be singing and dancing?"

"Yes, but you have to sit so other people can see. If I count you to 3 for standing up and dancing, you'll have to leave."

Rita does fine for three minutes, then stands up.

"Rita, that's 1. At 3 you will have to leave."

How Did She Do?

This approach is much better. The only caveat is that the teacher will need to know ahead of time what she will do with Rita once they have left the assembly. Is it a time-out in the hall while another teacher watches the class, or is it a visit to the office?

Teasing

Michael has another student cornered on the playground and is calling him names. The teacher intervenes.

"Michael, teasing is not OK; you need to stop."
(Michael continues.)
"That's 1."
"No! He started it and now it's my turn."
"That's 2."
"I am only doing what he did to me!" *(Continues the torturing.)*
"That's 3. Take five on the bench."
(Michael storms over to the bench to serve his time.)

How Did He Do?

Couldn't have done it better.

Getting to Work

It's time for journal writing. Alex is reading a library book.

"Alex, it's time to get to work on your journal."
(Entranced with his book, Alex does not respond at all.)
"Alex, that's 1."

How Did She Do?

This one is a little tricky. Should counting be used for getting students to do their work? In a sense, the answer is no, because journal writing is a Start behavior, which will very likely take more than just two minutes. Counting is usually for controlling obnoxious or difficult behavior, such as whining, arguing, or teasing, where cooperation takes only a few seconds.

Some astute teachers have pointed out, however, that as soon as this teacher said it was time for journal writing, the student's reading a library book actually became a Stop behavior. It was no longer appropriate, and therefore counting could be used to get the child to put the library book down. This is a valid point. One caution: journal writing is still a prolonged Start behavior, so the teacher should keep in mind other Start behavior tactics, such as praise, to help keep the writing going.

Requests

Eight-year-old Tom asks his teacher if he can use the computer.

"Not right now. I need you to finish your math."

"Oh come on, you let me do it yesterday."

"No, that was yesterday and this is today."

"I don't know how to do this math. I'm stupid." (badgering, martyrdom)

"I said no. That's 1."

"THAT'S 1! THAT'S 2! THAT'S 3! THAT'S 12! THAT'S 20! THAT'S STUPID!" (intimidation)

"That's 2."

"Didn't know you could count that high." (intimidation)

"That's 3, take 10 and add 5 for the mouth."

"Gee, I'll need a calculator for this one."

The teacher walks away before she says something she will regret and goes to compliment another student who is working on her math. Tom thinks about it for a minute and then slowly walks to time-out.

How Did She Do?

The teacher did very well; one explanation and then she counted. She also adds five for the smart mouth, and she has the presence of mind to stay cool in spite of the insult. When Tom doesn't go to time-out right away, she also does not get caught up in an argument or Little Adult conversation.

Interrupting

Round One

The principal comes in to let the teacher know that there will be a hurricane drill later in the afternoon and wants to explain the procedure to her without the students overhearing. The students are watching a ten-minute science video so she has a moment to speak with him.

During the conversation, a second-grader, Michelle, comes up to tell the principal that he forgot to announce her birthday during morning announcements.

"Excuse me, but I need to talk to the principal."

"Not now, Michelle, we are having a private conversation."

"I can stand here and wait until you are done. I promise I won't listen."

"No, dear. Please go back to your desk."

"This is really important! It's about my birthday." (badgering)

"I'm not going to tell you again!"

"I have to talk to him, and I've already seen this video!" (intimidation)

"Did you hear what I said?"

(Michelle starts crying.) (martyrdom)

"OK, that's 1."

(Michelle leaves, crying.)

How Did She Do?

This is a pretty sloppy job by the teacher. In all fairness, this is a touchy situation because Michelle's entrance is very friendly, and it is her birthday, after all. The teacher gets around to counting only after ridiculous attempts at persuasion and threatening. She eventually recovers and counts, but some damage has still been done.

Round Two

Let's take it from the top and give this teacher a second chance:

"Excuse me, but I need to talk to the principal."

"Not now, Michelle, we are having a private conversation."

"I can stand here and wait until you are done. I promise I won't listen."

"That's 1."

"This is really important! It's about my birthday." (badgering)

"That's 2."

(Michelle leaves, a bit teary.)

How Did She Do?

The teacher may feel a little guilty, but she handled the situation well. You can't give kids everything they want. Most likely the principal will realize the oversight and take care of it later, and we don't want Michelle to learn to interrupt to get her way.

Talking in Class

During geography, Sally and Marci start a conversation across the aisle. Mrs. Smith stops her discussion of crops in Argentina.

"Girls, I need your attention."

(The girls stop talking for thirty seconds, but then can't resist finishing what they started.)

"Sally, Marci, that's 1."

(The girls stop talking.)

How Did She Do?

Crisp and to the point. Easier on the children's self-esteem than a lot of self-righteous criticism. Counting in a situation like this also does not break the flow of instruction.

Arguing

As Mr. Britton is setting up for the science experiment, eleven-year-old Jeff asks:

"Can I go check lost and found for my jacket?"

"No, we are about to do a science experiment," says Mr. Britton.

"I'll be really quick."

"That's what you said last time, and you took forever. Remember?"

"Oh, please. I promise!" (badgering, butter up)

"Do this lesson first, and then you can go. If you work hard, it shouldn't take long."

"Why can't I just go now!? I'll DO MY STUPID WORK LATER!" (intimidation)

"That's 1."

"I can't wait to grow up so I can become an adult and make all the rules. It stinks being a kid." (martyrdom)

"That's 2."

"All right, all right, all right." *(Jeff goes to start the experiment.)*

How Did He Do?

The teacher did very well here. He tried a little negotiating, but when that didn't work, he didn't get caught up in a useless argument or try to explain that even adults have to follow rules they don't like sometimes.

To Share or Not to Share

Haley and Alyssa are four-year-olds. Unfortunately, everything Alyssa touches, Haley tries to take away from her. Alyssa is not aggressive at all, but just stands there looking bewildered after a toy has been taken from her hands.

The teacher sees the pattern. Alyssa picks up a small red car. Haley moves in and grabs it. The teacher says:

"Haley, that's 1. You must let Alyssa play with something."
(Haley still doesn't let go.)
"Haley, that's 2."
(The little girl releases her hold and lets Alyssa have the car.)
"That's very nice of you, sweetheart."

How Did She Do?

Good job. Explain, count, and praise cooperation.

Conclusion

What have our tales from the trenches taught us? Kids can certainly catch you off guard, for one thing! You have to be on your toes and—to be fair to yourself and the children—you have to make reasonable and fairly rapid decisions about which offenses are countable and which are not. Good counting takes a little bit of practice, but once you master the skill, you'll wonder how you ever got along without this sanity-saving technique.

CHAPTER SUMMARY
Is it magic?

The "magic" of the 1-2-3 procedure is not in the counting itself. The power of the method comes primarily from your ability to accomplish two goals. Your first objective is to explain—when necessary—and then keep quiet. Your second objective is to count as calmly and unemotionally as you can.

Do these two things well, and your students will start listening to you!

12

MORE SERIOUS OFFENSES

How to Handle Serious Discipline Issues in the Classroom

OLDER KIDS AND PRETEENS sometimes do things that fall into the category of Stop behavior, but their actions are too serious for our counting and time-out procedures. Included in this worrisome list of childhood exploits are lying, stealing, fighting (physical), bullying, damaging property, pulling pranks, smoking, and starting fires. Stronger but non-abusive action is now required, and usually, so is parent contact. Make sure to know your school policies about such offenses.

Some normal preadolescent children, especially boys, engage in isolated incidents that include the unusual and harmful activities listed above. Sometimes these kids are influenced by other children to do things they wouldn't otherwise do. Exercising temporary poor judgment, these youngsters are going along for the ride. When the response is a firm hand and a fair punishment, these first-time offenders tend to not become repeat offenders. This chapter will help you deal with such children and such incidents.

Other times, however, the trouble-producing motivation comes from inside the child himself. When a child starts showing a pattern of unusually hostile, aggressive, rule-breaking behavior, we begin to worry—especially as the youngster gets older. That's why we are so interested in early prevention: the older they are, the harder kids are to change. This chapter will help you manage more upsetting childhood behavior reasonably, firmly, and calmly.

Most teachers and parents will not need to use this chapter a lot—or perhaps even at all. But when it is necessary, the kind of targeted, rational management described here is essential in preventing the problem behavior of vulnerable, higher-risk children from escalating as they grow up.

Oppositional Defiance and Conduct Disorder

Although we do not totally understand why some children (mostly boys) start down a destructive and antisocial path of behavior, we do know a few things. Two motives that have been implicated in the more serious behavioral problems we just listed are (1) hostile and vengeful inclinations and (2) thrill seeking. Hostile or vengeful impulses, for example, may drive behavior such as fighting, bullying, and damaging property. Thrill seeking may be involved in smoking or starting fires. Many problem behaviors, of course, can involve both motives. When this is the case, the reinforcement a young lad gets from engaging in a "double-motive" activity can be even more powerful and dangerous.

Adolescents and preteens who consistently engage in aggressive, destructive, rule-breaking behavior that hurts others or damages property are often diagnosed with conduct disorder (CD). Remember, the diagnosis is made outside of school by a medical or mental health professional. The troublesome activities of kids with CD often reflect the two motives of hostile aggression and thrill seeking. These children may also have problems with learning difficulties, attention deficit disorder, language and communication, and the ability to read social cues. In addition, the parental supervision these children receive is often inconsistent, varying from overly hostile to nonexistent.

Preadolescents who sometimes seem to get addicted to hostile and vengeful behavior are often referred to as having oppositional defiant disorder (ODD). While youths with CD may want to hurt others, kids with ODD simply like to aggravate you. Kids with ODD are negative, defiant, and can't take no for answer. They deliberately annoy other people, are in turn easily annoyed themselves, and blame everybody else for anything that goes wrong.

ODD probably has some genetic basis, but this disorder can also be caused—as well as seriously aggravated—by sloppy, inconsistent, angry, and overly wordy parenting. In any case, ODD behavior usually starts at home during the preschool years. And when poor parenting is part of the picture, oppositional-defiant kids can graduate to become conduct-disorder kids; they simply take their troublesome behavior out of the house and into the school and community. Teens with CD can be dangerous kids with treacherous futures.

One of the goals of *1-2-3 Magic in the Classroom* is to prevent oppositional defiance from starting in the first place by means of reasonable, gentle, and solid discipline. A second goal of *1-2-3 Magic* is to eliminate early ODD behavior problems—once they have started—so they don't evolve into CD. Get rid of early ODD and you cut the risk of later trouble tremendously.

For most kids who are not at risk for major ODD problems, the basic 1-2-3 Magic program will probably be sufficient for discipline purposes. With higher-risk children who start engaging in more serious problem behavior, however, parents and teachers will need to also pay particular attention to what we call the Major/Minor System. With these more risky youngsters, it is also critical that the same, consistent discipline procedures be used both at home and at school.

Quick Tip

Two motives that have been implicated in kids' destructive and antisocial behavior are (1) hostile, vengeful inclinations and (2) thrill seeking. These children often have other problems, such as learning difficulties, attention deficit disorder, language deficits, and difficulty reading social cues.

The Major/Minor System

The teacher next door, Mr. Jones, comes by your room, and he is furious. He lets you know that one of your students, Russell, has just ripped down part of a hall display that took weeks to create and hours to put up. He wants to know what you're going to do about it and how you're going to punish the kid.

You are shocked, embarrassed, and incredulous. You apologize to your aggravated colleague and tell him you'll certainly take care of it. Russell isn't a "problem child," but you know he's had a few run-ins with this teacher, who does tend to be a real grouch sometimes. If your student did destroy the display, that would obviously be Stop behavior. However, it wouldn't make much sense to run up to him and say, "Russell, that's 1." "That's 3, take five, and add 15 for the seriousness of the offense" would also seem too mild. Some punishment may be called for, but even then, you still want to avoid a lot of the excess talking and emotion that will only make things worse.

Fortunately, there is a very simple punishment system that you can set up to handle serious problems like this with a minimum of upset and confusion. It's called the Major/Minor System. With the Major/Minor System, you will establish appropriate Major or Minor punishments/consequences for corresponding Major or Minor offenses. The Major/Minor System is applied differently, depending upon how much trouble you've had in the past with a particular child. Is this the first time that you've had a serious problem with this child, or have there been repeated episodes?

> **Quick Tip**
>
> There is a very simple punishment system you can set up to handle more serious problems like lying, stealing, fighting, and destroying property. With the Major/Minor System, you set up Major or Minor punishments, or consequences, for Major or Minor offenses.

First-Time Offenses

With first-time offenses, like Russell in our previous example, you only need to deal with the problem at hand. You do not need to make a big list of behavior issues and punishments like you may do with repeated problems.

So let's imagine that after your irate colleague leaves, you track down Russell. You tell him about your conversation with Mr. Jones. Then you ask him what happened. You remain calm and "put on your sympathetic listening shoes" (see chapter 21). Russell is not a bad kid, and you're determined to hear him out first, and then determine what needs to be done.

Russell tells you that he was walking back from the bathroom and was looking at the display. A student from Mr. Jones' class came up to him and started teasing him. "Russell the dummy...you couldn't do a project like mine in a million years, you're so stupid. So stop staring and keep walking." Russell explains that he was upset and just wanted to get back at that student by ripping her project down. But he was so mad that once he started, he couldn't stop.

How should you apply the Major/Minor System? Tell your student that even though he was teased, he exercised poor judgment during the incident by letting his own temper get the best of him. Russell is therefore going to have to accept several consequences, and the consequences here will not involve time-out. First, the boy will go back and tell Mr. Jones that he, Russell, will clean up the mess and repair what he can. You also tell Russell that he needs to write a letter to the class accepting responsibility for his actions, and he must also take this letter home and present it to his parents.

This punishment constitutes a major consequence for Russell. Your assignment will be no small chore for the young lad. Russell does as instructed, though, and the problem is resolved. You tell him you're proud of him and the way he took responsibility for his actions. No other consequences or lectures are necessary. You may want to talk to Russell's parents and tell them what consequences were delivered at school.

By the way, as the adult here, you did a good job, too. You did not beat down your pupil because you were embarrassed by his behavior.

Repeat Offenses

What if, on the other hand, you've had a number of more serious problems with your fifth-grade pupil Mike? In the last several months, Mike's been late to class three times (you think maybe on purpose). You also think he smells like he's been smoking a few times, and you're never sure if he's lying about his homework. Mike's grades have slipped from a B+ to a C+ average in the last two quarters. He also seems less interested in talking with you or with other students.

When kids start acting up like this, it's easy to get so irritated that all you can think of is doling out punishment. When the child does something right, you ignore the good deed and think, "Well, it's about time!" When he does something wrong, however, you angrily jump all over him. This defensive and aggressive stance on your part runs the risk of making the child so angry that he is more likely to engage in vengeful and hostile—as well as perhaps thrill-seeking—behavior. The reaction and counterreaction sequence can be the start of an in-school war between you and him, with the result being that the child's future is in much greater jeopardy. Instead of that unproductive, knee-jerk type of reaction, your strategy with Mike should involve two primary lines of attack: (1) improving your relationship with him through regular doses of praise, fun, and forgiveness (chapter 20) and sympathetic listening (chapter 21); and (2) setting up a Major/Minor System.

We'll discuss how to improve a relationship with a child more specifically in Part VI. Here we'll focus on the Major/Minor System. You will set up a well-defined system of behavioral consequences for Mike. The consequences chosen for each offense will depend on the seriousness of the behavior involved, varying from major offenses to minor transgressions. (Minor offenses here are still more serious than countable problems.) The corresponding list of major and minor consequences may include variations of detention, fines, chores, service, or educational activities. Refer to the following examples.

MAJOR CONSEQUENCES

Detention: seven days staying after school for 45 minutes
Fine: loss of 25 classroom tokens (if token economy system is used)
Chores: twelve hours' work in the classroom
Service: twelve hours' work in the school
Educational activity: research subject (e.g., smoking) and write quality five-page paper

MINOR CONSEQUENCES

Detention: three days staying after school for 45 minutes
Fine: loss of ten tokens (if token economy system is used)
Chores: four hours' work in the classroom
Service: four hours' work in the school
Educational activity: research subject (e.g., bad language) and write quality two-page paper

As you can see, the punishments for major offenses are greater than the punishments for minor problems. The above ideas are only suggestions: individual teachers and administrators can certainly alter these guidelines. Over the years, we have learned that there will always be some people who think we are too strict, and others who think we are not strict enough when it comes to more serious behavior! Keep in mind that even the minor offenses described in this chapter are still more serious than countable things such as arguing, yelling, teasing, whining, and so on.

Once you have come up with your punishment classifications, you decide which behavior merits which class of punishment. When that misbehavior occurs, one of the consequences from the list is

Quick Tip

Once the Major/Minor System is set up, when a student pulls a fast one, you simply categorize it and determine the consequence. No yelling or lecturing is allowed, although short discussions may sometimes help.

implemented—not the whole list! This process saves a lot of effort and deliberation and also lets your youngster know the consequences beforehand if he decides to mess up. Some teachers even let the child choose the consequence, once the Major or Minor category has been chosen.

Recall that Mike was acting up more in the last few months. After reviewing the school's policies, you work out the following classifications with Mike:

MAJOR OFFENSES

Coming to class more than fifteen minutes late
Smoking
Lying about more serious matters

MINOR OFFENSES

Coming to class less than fifteen minutes late
Lying about homework

Have Mike bring the list of misbehaviors and consequences home to discuss with his parents. Once the system is set up, when Mike pulls a fast one, you simply categorize it and determine the consequence. No yelling or screaming by you is allowed, of course, although a short explanation or discussion may occasionally be in order (see chapter 19). What if the youngster does something that you didn't put on the original Major/Minor list? You just classify it as Major or Minor and then pick a punishment.

You can adjust the Major/Minor System after you set it up, but be careful not to make punishments so harsh that they backfire. A twenty-page paper or detentions for a month are probably bad ideas. Discipline like this will not work because (1) it becomes very difficult to enforce and (2) it will probably start a long-term war between you and your student.

If you've been having a serious problem with repeated offenses, you can also make a chart that keeps track of the number of days in a row during which the child stays free of trouble. There might even be a reward for this good performance, such as a special privilege. If serious problems continue in spite of the Major/Minor System— and in spite of your working to improve your relationship with the youngster—it is probably time to meet with the parents and other members of the educational team.

Several other prevention-oriented thoughts are in order here. If you have a young lad who seems inclined along ODD/CD lines, research has shown that there are a number of important factors that can help prevent future problems. And some of these factors may be worth discussing with the child's parents. These problem-reducing factors include day-to-day discipline consistency, discipline consistency between parents, discipline consistency and coordination between home and school, and close—but reasonable—supervision of the child. You might want to consult the school psychologist or social worker before trying to talk things over with Mom and Dad.

Lying

The problem of children lying is included in this chapter for two reasons: (1) lying itself is a more serious offense; and (2) lying is often used to cover up other more serious offenses. Lying drives some teachers crazy, and managing this problem is often confusing and difficult. Therefore, we'll try to provide some basic guidelines.

There are basically two kinds of lies. The first kind involves making up stories that are designed to impress other people and build up one's ego. One little boy, for example, told his classmates about his riding elephants in India while hunting tigers. This type of verbal fabrication is not so common in children.

The second kind, and by far the most common, is telling falsehoods to avoid trouble. This type may involve covering up a past misdeed or trying to get out of some unpleasant task. Kids who steal, for example, will almost always lie about the theft when they are initially confronted. Other kids lie about having their work finished so they won't have to face a boring job.

When it comes to dealing with lying, the first thing to remember is not to treat the act as if it were the equivalent of grand larceny. Not telling the truth certainly isn't a good thing, but it's not a truly terrible behavior. Many teachers get so upset about lying that they act as though the world were coming to an end. Consequently, these grown-ups lead students to believe that they are horrible people for having lied.

What Should You Do about Lying?

One day you see a student take a calculator off your desk and put it in his own desk. You are surprised, angered, and bewildered. You later approach the boy and start a conversation like this:

"How's it going?"

"Good. I'm glad I got a B on my math test."

"Speaking of math, have you seen my calculator?"

"No, where do you keep it?"

"On my desk."

"What color is it?"

"OK, listen, young man. You're lying to me. I saw you take it."

In this conversation, the teacher is "cornering" the youngster. Sure, she wants to get some information, but first the teacher wants to test the boy to see if he'll tell the truth. Is this the right way to handle the situation? The answer is no.

When you know some kind of trouble has occurred, don't corner children. When you corner a child, you give him a chance to practice lying. You may think to yourself, "Sooner or later he'll realize he can't fool me, and he'll give up the charade." Sometimes kids do give up during an interrogation, but many children will continue trying to take the easy way out first. They will simply work to become better liars, and you will be helping to provide them with their practice sessions.

Here's a more constructive approach. Imagine something bad has happened. You either know the truth or you don't. If you don't know what occurred, ask the youngster once what happened. If he tells you the story and you find out later that the child lied, punish him for whatever the original offense was and, using the Major/Minor System, for the lie as well.

Also, try not to surprise the child by asking your questions "impulsively," or on the spur of the moment. Many kids will simply respond back impulsively. They'll lie, but their real desire is just to end the conversation, get rid of you, and stay out of trouble. For example, imagine something bad has happened and you already know all the gory details. You might say something like this to a student: "I want you to tell me the story of what happened

> **Quick Tip**
> When talking to a student about a questionable incident, try to avoid "cornering" the child. Cornering the youngster to see if he'll tell the truth often has the long-term effect of simply producing a More Accomplished Liar.

at lunch today, but not right now. Think about it a while and we'll talk in fifteen minutes. But remember, I already talked with the lunch monitor." No lectures or tantrums from you.

There is another option many adults use when (1) they already know what happened and (2) the child is very likely to lie about the event no matter how the questions are phrased. In this case you simply tell the youngster what you know and then calmly mete out the punishment. You do not even give the child the chance to lie. This is what the teacher whose calculator was taken should have done. When confronted like this, some kids will still blow up and accuse you of not trusting them (testing tactic 2, temper). Manage the testing by ignoring their statement or counting them, and end the conversation with, "I'm sure you'll do better next time."

When you have a child who uses lying regularly to avoid unpleasant tasks, such as schoolwork or classroom chores, try also to fix the problem—as much as you can—so that lying does not seem necessary to the child. If your student continually lies about having his homework finished, for example, work out some kind of written communication, such as a daily assignment sheet. For classroom jobs, consider fixing the problem by the judicious use of other Start behavior strategies (see chapter 13).

> **Quick Tip**
>
> When you have a child who uses lying regularly to avoid unpleasant tasks, try to fix the problem as much as you can so that lying does not seem necessary to the child.

Lying is not good, but it certainly isn't the end of the world either. Most people, children as well as adults, probably tell a few "stretchers" from time to time. Not telling the truth doesn't mean that a student is bound to end up as an inmate in a federal penitentiary. Lying is a problem, though, and it needs to be managed carefully and thoughtfully. Over the years, frequent emotional overreactions from adults—combined with badgering and cornering—can help produce Accomplished Liars.

Congratulations! You have just learned classroom discipline Step 1: Managing Undesirable Behavior. You are ready to begin counting, and you are prepared for any testing and manipulation from your students. So now we're on to the next giant step: Encouraging Good Behavior.

CHAPTER SUMMARY

1. A principle goal of the Major/Minor System is the prevention of bigger behavior problems later on.
2. Many teachers won't ever need to use this part of our program.
3. Use the Major/Minor System for more serious problems, such as stealing, bullying, damaging property, violating hours, and lying.
4. When implementing consequences, be decisive and—although it's very hard—be as calm and reasonable as you can!

⁞⁞⁞⁞ PART IV ⁞⁞⁞⁞

Encouraging Good Behavior

Classroom Discipline Step 2

CHAPTER 13
Establishing Positive Routines

CHAPTER 14
Using 1-2-3 Magic When Your Class Is on the Move

CHAPTER 15
Coordinating Arrival, Dismissal, and Transitions

CHAPTER 16
Completing Classroom Jobs and Chores

CHAPTER 17
Getting the Schoolwork Done

CHAPTER 18
Conducting Class Meetings

CHAPTER 19
Discussing Behavior Issues with Your Students

13

ESTABLISHING
POSITIVE ROUTINES

How to Motivate Your Students to
Do the Things They Need to Do

NOW WE TURN OUR attention to the second big discipline step: encouraging children to do the positive things you want them to do. We call this behavior category Start behavior because you want your students to start doing their schoolwork, lining up, paying attention, cleaning their desks, and transitioning smoothly from one activity to the next.

Recall that children's cooperation with Start behavior requires more motivation from them than cooperation when Stop behavior is involved. While it may only take one second to stop talking, running in the hallway, or arguing, tasks such as schoolwork may require twenty minutes or more. Kids not only have to start these jobs, they also have to continue and finish them. Counting difficult behavior to make it stop is fairly simple. When it comes to encouraging positive behavior, however, adults have to be more skilled and persistent motivators.

If your classroom feels completely out of control when beginning this program, it might be a good idea to use counting first for a week to ten days before tackling our Start behavior methods. If you try to do the whole program at once (both Stop and Start problems), it may be a little too much to keep straight. Equally important, it will also be considerably easier to get the kids to do the good things if you have first gotten back in control of the classroom by effectively managing their obnoxious conduct. On the other hand, if things are going relatively well at this point and you simply want to add 1-2-3 Magic to your classroom procedures, you may wish to begin with the combination of Stop and Start behavior strategies. In fact, since Start behavior tactics come naturally to many teachers, you may already be using some of these ideas.

When you begin using your Start behavior tactics, don't be surprised if you run into some testing and manipulation from your students. Remember, they are not going to thank you for asking them to clean up or complete other boring or unpleasant tasks. If you have worked on counting negative behavior first, you will have had a fair amount of experience in dealing with Stop behavior, such as testing, before you tackle the task of getting the kids to do the good things. So have the 1-2-3 process ready in your back pocket so you can pull that tool out whenever necessary.

We will describe eight Start behavior tactics. Sometimes you may use just one tactic, but other times you may use two or three for the same problem. While counting undesirable behavior is fairly straightforward, you can be more creative and flexible when encouraging positive behavior. In fact, many teachers and parents have come up with useful and imaginative ideas of their own that are not on our list.

Quick Tip

For Start behavior, you can use more than one tactic at a time for a particular problem. You can also change tactics when necessary. Remember that your job is to train the kids to do what you want, which can take time.

Wonderful, Powerful Routines!

Many people think the word *routine* means bad and boring. You will soon learn that when it comes to Start behavior, routines are wonderful and powerful. Learning how to complete activities like lining up and completing classroom chores are complex and take time. Kids have to learn to regularly follow a fixed sequence of actions. Same time, same place, same way. Once a routine is mastered, kids tend to do it automatically.

Routines for positive behavior drastically reduce your discipline problems, and they can also make testing and manipulation virtually nonexistent. We'll discuss more about how to establish routines at the end of this chapter.

The Eight Start Behavior Tactics

There are eight Start behavior tactics you can consider using to establish and maintain your routines. Sometimes you may use just one tactic, but other times you may use two or three for the same problem. While counting obnoxious behavior is fairly straightforward, you can be more creative and flexible when managing positive behavior. In fact, many parents and teachers have come up with useful and imaginative ideas that are not on our list.

Here are our eight tactics for encouraging good behavior:

1. Positive reinforcement
2. Simple requests
3. Kitchen timers
4. The docking system
5. Natural consequences
6. Charting
7. Counting for brief Start behavior
8. Cross dialogue

When dealing with Start behavior, keep in mind one of the basic rules of 1-2-3 Magic: train the children or keep quiet! In the 1-2-3 program, there is a method for handling just about every kind of problem your pupils can throw at you. So use these methods! For example, kids are not born to be natural cleaner-uppers. If the child isn't cleaning out his desk, train him to do it. Otherwise, be quiet, clean it yourself, or don't bother looking at the mess. Training, however, does not mean nagging, arguing, or yelling.

With these rules in mind, let's take a look at the eight tactics you will use to get the kids to do what they're supposed to do.

1. Positive Reinforcement

Why is there a "home-field advantage" in sports? It's because the crowd encourages the home team by cheering and applauding. Even for professional athletes, this type of praise is a strong motivator. Unfortunately, this home-field-advantage effect doesn't always translate from stadium to classroom. Why?

Angry people make noise; happy people keep quiet. We all suffer from a biological curse that motivates us to say something to kids when we're angry with them, but to keep quiet when the little ones are doing what we want them to do. Imagine it's the first time all day that your students have been working quietly. This gives you a few minutes to grade a couple of papers and respond to an urgent email from a parent. What are the chances that you will stop what you are doing to praise the class for working quietly? That would be a great thing to do, but the chances of your doing it may be low. Why? Because when adults are happy and content themselves, they are not particularly motivated to do anything more than what they're already doing.

But imagine that two children across the room start teasing and fighting. Why do they behave this way?! Now you are motivated— you're mad. And now the chances of you getting up, running over to the two offenders, and yelling at them to keep quiet are high. Anger is a much better motivator than contentment. The result is that kids are more likely to hear from us when we have negative rather than positive feedback.

One powerful antidote to this unfortunate natural inclination is praise, or positive verbal reinforcement. Praise should be given early and often, every day. Your praise and other positive interactions with your students should outnumber your negative comments by a ratio of about three to

Key Concept

Angry people make noise; happy people keep quiet.

one. If you look, you shouldn't have trouble finding some positive behavior to reinforce:

"Thanks for passing out the papers."

"You started your work all by yourself! Wonderful!"

"Your reading buddy really likes you."

"You guys did a good job of getting along during recess today."

"I think you got ready for science in record time this morning!"

"Good job on that math test, John."

"I saw you out on the soccer field. You played hard—good hustle!"

"That's terrific! I knew you could do it!"

Once you have the kids successfully carrying out a particular Start behavior, positive reinforcement can help keep the cooperation or good performance going. Many teachers, for example, praise or thank their kids for complying with simple requests or for following a routine.

Keep a sensitive eye on your boys and girls, though, because praise should be tailored to some extent for each child and each situation. Some kids like rather elaborate, syrupy, and emotional verbal reinforcement, while others do not. Imagine your second grader gets 100 percent on her spelling test for the first time all year. You say, "Oh, Melissa, that's just marvelous! I can't believe it! We're going to put this on the 'Good Work' board and show it to the principal." Melissa eats it up.

Melissa's classmate Jason, however, would be nauseated by that kind of talk. For him, "Good job—keep up the good work," and a pat on the shoulder might be enough. Your job is to praise the child, not to embarrass him.

Two additional tricks can help make praise a more effective boost to a child's self-esteem:

1. Give praise in front of other people
2. Offer unexpected praise

For example, while you're talking to another teacher, Kelsey walks up. You interrupt your conversation and say, "You should have seen Kelsey in the library today; she was so polite and helpful!" Kelsey will beam with pride. Unexpected praise can also be done "across the room." Praising a child from way across the room is a powerful technique, not only because it is unexpected, but also because it gives all students the sense that the teacher sees everything that's going on.

> **Quick Tip**
> Are we spoiling our kids with superficial, phony praise? Basically, you can give elaborate praise to kids younger than seven—they likely can't tell the difference between fake and genuine praise. Once kids get older than that, though, it's best to dial back on the praise and make sure that you're giving them only genuine, heartfelt compliments.

Unexpected praise can also be quite memorable for a child. What do students usually expect when you call them over or out into the hall? They expect that they are in trouble, right? Are they going to be motivated to come to you when you ask? Of course not. One way you can increase the odds that a student will come when you call them, however, is to keep them guessing. Sometimes you will need to talk with him about a problem. Other times, though, you will give him a compliment. For example, you call to a student from across the room, "Hey, Jordan! Please come here, I need to talk with you." Jordan has no idea what's coming next, and he anticipates the worst. You then say, "Did I tell you what a great job you did on your social studies project?" Jordan will be pleased and perhaps more than a little relieved!

How do you keep offering praise and encouragement on a regular basis? As mentioned before, this task is surprisingly difficult, since most of us don't think to comment when we are content. Here are two suggestions. First, see if you can make three positive comments for every one negative comment (by the way, one count is one negative comment). These positive remarks don't have to be made at the same time, of course. They can be made later. If the three-to-one ratio doesn't appeal to you, a second strategy is to have a quota system. Each day you make a deal with yourself that you will make at least two positive comments to each child.

One paraeducator was feeling challenged to praise a group of students with particularly difficult behavior. She decided to put ten pennies in her right pocket at the beginning of each lesson or activity. For each positive comment she made to a student or the group, she moved a penny to the left pocket. Her goal was to move all ten pennies to the left by the end of each period. This way, she ended up making at least one hundred positive comments a day! Better yet, after a while it became a habit and she no longer needed the pennies at all.

Another version of positive reinforcement is praising other students for doing the right thing in order to motivate others to join him or her in the good behavior. This tactic is sometimes called "next door" praise. If Joe is rummaging through his desk, but Marcus, who sits right next to Joe, is looking at you during your lecture, you would say, "I like the way you are making eye contact, Marcus; that shows me you are ready for the next direction." Some teachers set up desks in table groups and either number them or name them. If table groups are set up, you could say, "I see tables 2, 4, and 5 are ready. Thank you for clearing your desks." Then watch the other tables scurry to do the same thing. Believe it or not, kids want to behave, so often an effective technique is to point out what children should be doing instead of nagging them about what they shouldn't be doing.

2. Simple Requests

The problem with simple requests is that they are not so simple. Requests to children can be made more or less effective by a teacher's tone of voice, the spontaneity of the request, and the phrasing of the demand. It has been said that over 90 percent of what we communicate is done nonverbally through body language and tone of voice. Several pieces of advice may be helpful.

WATCH THAT VOICE!

We all have different voices. The voice we're concerned about here is often called our "nagging voice." The nagging voice has a "You're not doing what I expect and it's really irritating and what's the matter with you and when are you going to learn" quality. A nagging voice has an aggravated and anxious tone that most children find irritating. When this tone of voice is coupled with a request, it makes cooperation less likely because you are now asking an angry child to cooperate with you.

A good antidote to the nagging voice is a businesslike, matter-of-fact presentation. "John, it is now time to start your work," or "Taylor, line up." This tone of voice implies, "You may not like this, but it's got to be done now." Testing is much less likely when requests are made in a matter-of-fact way, but—believe it or not—the mere tone of voice can also say, "If you test or push me, you'll get counted."

KEEP REQUESTS SHORT

Keeping the request short (three words or less) can also encourage compliance. With some students, using one-step directions with as few words as possible can make all the difference. For example, suppose Tricia, who has oppositional behavior to begin with, hears this request: "Now Tricia, I want you to stop talking, pick up your things, and move to the back table. I have had enough of your disruptions. Maybe sitting away from the group will help." Tricia is not likely to follow along because the wordiness of the teacher's request is confusing and invites a power struggle. It may be easier for this little girl to argue with the teacher and end up in time-out than to try to sort out the long, convoluted direction she was just given.

A better approach would be for the teacher to say, "Tricia, back table." After all, the teacher's goal is to minimize the disruption. If Tricia moves, the talking will cease. Someone else can bring her materials or Tricia may do it automatically.

SPONTANEITY IS DANGEROUS

Although often unavoidable, the spontaneity of a request can also be a cooperation killer. Let's say that music class was canceled for the day but you forgot to note it on the posted schedule. The students were looking forward to music at 1:00, but when that time comes, you let them know that instead of going to music, it is time to clean out their desks. The students moan, groan, and complain.

No one likes spur-of-the-moment interruptions that involve unpleasant tasks. You don't like them either, but you are often stuck with such intrusions. But we're not talking about getting you to cooperate here; we're talking about getting your pupils to cooperate. And we're also not saying children shouldn't have jobs to do. They *should* help out around the classroom. The point is this: try to structure tasks so that spontaneous requests are seldom necessary. In the situation just mentioned, it would have been helpful to make the change (music to desk cleaning) on the schedule at the beginning of the day, so students could get used to the idea of desk cleaning rather than having it "sprung" on them at the last minute.

EFFECTIVE PHRASING

Finally, the phrasing of a request can also make a difference in how kids respond. Phrasing a request as a question and adding the often ridiculous "we" to the statement will often ensure noncompliance or testing and manipulation. A super-sweet "Don't we think it's about time to start our work?" is almost guaranteed to elicit a negative response. In general it is very dangerous to make requests in the form of a question. "Do you want me to call your parents?" or "Do you want to stay after school today?" might receive a "Yes" from a provocative and oppositional student. A better way of phrasing the work request would be, "I want your journal entry complete by lunchtime."

What if, in spite of everything, your simple request still does no good? We'll come back to that question after we've discussed several other Start behavior options.

3. Kitchen Timers

Kitchen timers are wonderful devices for encouraging good behavior in children. Many kinds are useful, including the sixty-minute wind-up variety as well as computer, small LCD, and even hourglass varieties. The people who manufacture timers think they're for baking cakes. They're not—timers are for assisting you with your class! Kitchen timers can be a great help for just about any

Start behavior, whether it's picking up, lining up, or transitioning. Kids, especially the younger ones, have a natural tendency to want to beat a ticking mechanical device. The problem then becomes a case of "man against machine" (rather than student against teacher).

These portable motivational gadgets can also be used, if you like, to time the time-outs themselves. Many kids actually prefer doing the time-out with a timer, but you may want to set up a "touch it and lose it" rule so students do not adjust the timer to shorten their time.

Timers can also soften the blow of unavoidable spontaneous requests. For example, the principal announces there will be a special visitor touring the building soon. You say to your class, "We've got to straighten up. I'm setting the timer for ten minutes. I'll bet you can't beat it!" The kids will respond, "Oh yes we can!" and the youngsters will be hurrying off to do the job. You could take this same approach to get older students to pick up, but you would phrase your request in a more matter-of-fact manner.

Kitchen timers are effective because they are not testable. Machines cannot be emotionally manipulated. Imagine that while Karl is taking a time-out, he is pouting and mumbling to himself, "This is stupid!" (testing tactics 2 and 4, temper and martyrdom). Your response is silence. The timer's response is *tick, tick, tick*.

4. The Docking System

The principle of docking wages is this: if you don't do the work, you don't get paid. The basic idea of the docking system is similar: if you don't do the work, you'll pay me. The docking system is for children who are kindergarten age or above.

This plan, of course, requires that you have some sort of token economy system in your classroom so your students have a source of funds. A token economy can work many different ways. Individual students can earn tokens, the whole group can earn them, or both. For tokens teachers have used stickers, plastic chips, marbles, laminated pieces of construction paper, and many other things. If you want to make this an academic activity as well, you can use plastic or paper money or a checkbook. Students are motivated to add up their "money," and they may not even realize that they are also practicing math skills at the same time.

The way tokens are distributed varies also. Some teachers distribute tokens throughout the day for specific behaviors, and others wait until the last period to reward a "good day." For some students and classes, just collecting tokens is motivation enough for kids to produce positive behavior. For others, however, the tokens need to be tied to an artificial reinforcer the student can "buy." Some teachers have "store time" every week, whereas others have an auction at the end of the year. Of course, the more money a student has, the more he can purchase.

The tokens, or "money," can be used to pay for things like jobs not done, broken property, or not taking a time-out. Of course, such fines would not be used if a child were not doing her schoolwork because kids should not be paying someone to do their schoolwork for them.

Let's say it is Michael's turn to feed the classroom guinea pig but he forgets to do his job on Tuesday afternoon. You have already explained to him that it is his job to remember. The good news is that if he forgets, you will do it for him. The bad news is he will owe you. Michael comes rushing in on Wednesday morning.

"Did you feed the guinea pig yesterday? I forgot."

"Yes, I did. I charged you three tokens from your account."

"WELL, WHAT DID YOU DO THAT FOR!?" (yelling)

"That's 1."

This is not a discussion. It was a discussion, but now it's an attack. It's simply one version of testing tactic 2, temper, and it should be counted. You discuss discussions and you count attacks. In this kind of situation, it's extremely difficult to resist the temptation to get into angry, Little Adult types of comments, such as, "Do you remember when I brought in the pet? What did the class agree to? You all said you would take turns feeding him. No problem! Right! Well, here we are on only the second week and I'm already feeding him! You guys need to learn to take some responsibility!"

> **Quick Tip**
>
> Avoid the temptation to argue with your students, even if you know you are right! Righteous indignation will do you no good.

What you're saying may be absolutely correct, but righteous indignation like this will do no good. Adult tantrums and lectures will, in fact, cause harm. Your tirade will do two things. First, the outburst will damage your relationship with the child. Second, your blowup will ruin the effect of the tokens the boy was docked. So be quiet and let the lost coins do the talking. If tokens don't seem to have much clout with this particular lad, take minutes off a preferred activity or use some other time-out alternative. Keep in mind, though, that no consequence works when the No Talking and No Emotion rules are being violated by the teacher.

Back to the docking system. The docking system can be used for lots of things. For example, have you ever said to your students, "I'm happy to grade your work; in fact, it is my job to do so. All you have to do is get your assignment to me on time. I am not going to hunt down your work, however. Either you turn it in or you don't."

Now let's imagine you're going to use the docking system for assignments not turned in. You say, "I'm happy to grade your work; in fact, it is my job to do so. All you have to do is get your assignment to me on time. If you forget your work in your locker, you can go get it, but I will charge you for the hall pass, and a hall pass in this situation is worth four tokens."

5. Natural Consequences

With natural consequences, you let the big, bad world teach the child what works and what doesn't. Though natural consequences have limited utility, there are times when your being uninvolved is the best approach.

One example of a natural consequence might be when a student refuses to sit quietly and keeps talking to his neighbor. The next time you give students two or three minutes to talk to each other during a transition between activities, that student would have to sit quietly while everyone else gets to talk. Another example is when a student does not bring her library books back and is consequently not allowed to check out other books. These are good "life lessons" for students.

As we saw before with little Rita dancing at the assembly, natural consequences can sometimes be combined with counting. For Rita, the natural consequence at the count of 3 was being removed from the assembly, one that she was enjoying.

Quick Tip

Don't forget to keep your counting strategy in your back pocket to back up your Start behavior procedures. Counting will come in very handy when your students decide to try arguing or whining about the positive things you want them to do.

6. Charting

Charting is a very friendly motivational technique. With charting, you use something like a calendar to keep track of how well a child is doing with different Start behaviors. You can put the chart on the child's desk, on a clipboard, or in a folder. The days of the week or periods in a day usually go across the top of the chart, and down the left side is a list of the tasks the child is working on, such as staying in her seat, completing her work, and not talking to other children. If the child completes the task to your satisfaction, you indicate this on the chart with stickers for the little kids (approximate ages four to nine) and numbers, points, or grades for the older children.

Here's what a chart might look like. This child is working on following directions the first time given; making smooth, quick transitions; and keeping quiet while doing schoolwork:

	Mon.	Tues.	Wed.	Thurs.	Fri.
Directions					
Transitions					
Quiet Work					

With charting, positive reinforcement for a child comes (we hope) from three things: the chart itself, praise from the teacher, and the inherent satisfaction of doing a good job. We call these three things natural reinforcers. If natural reinforcers are enough to elicit cooperation, stop there. The goal is to help the child develop intrinsic motivation rather than being motivated only by an extrinsic reward—what she "gets out of it."

Sometimes, however, natural reinforcers may not be enough to motivate a child to complete a particular task. In these cases you can use what we call artificial reinforcers. Artificial reinforcers mean that the child is going to earn something—which may have nothing directly to do with the task—for successful completion of that job. Since the activity doesn't provide any incentive to the child—and, in fact, may provide a negative incentive—we are going to try to borrow motivation from somewhere else. A girl who hates cleaning out her desk, for example, might earn tokens or a special time with you after keeping her desk clean for a month.

For smaller children, the best ideas are often relatively small things that can be given out frequently and in little pieces. With older kids, larger rewards that take longer to earn become more feasible. Let yourself be creative in coming up with reinforcers. Rewards certainly do not always have to be material. Some kids, for example, will work hard to earn extra minutes of a preferred activity.

Potential Artificial Reinforcers

- Brightly colored tokens
- Extra preferred activity time
- Stickers, happy faces
- Playing a special game
- A grab-bag surprise
- A book to take home over the weekend
- Choice of one of three reinforcers
- Playing a game with the principal
- Reading a story with a special adult
- A homework pass
- A snack

Keep charts simple. Two to four things to work on at one time is enough; more than that gets too confusing. If you try to rate twenty behaviors a day, you and the student will become frustrated and confused.

Keep in mind that you probably will not want to do charting for long periods of time (months and months). Charting can become a somewhat overwhelming behavioral accounting task, and the positive effects will fade if the teacher does not have enough time to fill out the chart every day. So build in discontinuation criteria—rules for determining when the chart is no longer necessary. You might say, for example, that if the child gets good scores (define this precisely) for two weeks straight on a particular behavior, then that item will be taken off the chart. When the child has earned his way off the chart entirely, it's time to celebrate! If after a while the child doesn't keep up with the desired behavior, you can reinstate the chart.

Quick Tip

You will probably not want to do charting for long periods of time, so build in discontinuation criteria—rules for determining when the chart is no longer necessary. When a pupil earns her way off the chart, celebrate!

7. Counting for Brief Start Behavior

As mentioned earlier, one of the most frequent mistakes adults make with the 1-2-3 program is attempting to use counting to get a child to do Start behavior like schoolwork, classroom jobs, or transitioning. Recall that these tasks can take twenty minutes or more, while counting itself only produces several seconds of motivation.

What if the Start behavior itself, however, requires only a few seconds of cooperation? Let's say you want your student to hang up her coat or come into the room quietly. Counting, which is so useful for Stop behavior, can be used for some Start behavior, but only on one condition: *what you want the child to do cannot take more than about two minutes.* For example, Tammy throws her coat on the floor, and you ask her to pick it up. She doesn't, and you say, "That's 1." If she still refuses to comply and gets timed out, she goes and serves the time. When she comes out, you say, "Please hang up your coat." If there is still no cooperation, another time-out would follow.

What if for some unknown reason this girl is in a totally ornery mood on that particular day, never seems to get the idea, and the coat

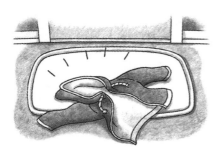

just lies there? With Start behavior tactics, you have more flexibility. With Tammy you might consider switching from counting to the docking system and the kitchen timer. Set the timer for five minutes and tell your student she has that time to hang up the coat. If she does pick it up, fine. You promise you won't say another word. If she doesn't hang it up, however, you have good news and bad news for her. You'll hang up the coat, but you will charge for your services. The charge will be two tokens for the coat and two tokens for all the aggravation that was just involved in trying to get her to hang it up. Keep the talking to a minimum, and count whining, arguing, yelling, and other forms of testing.

What else can you use this different version of the 1-2-3 program for? How about "Would you please come here for a second?" Imagine you need some help and you see Tim staring off into space. You say, "Tim, please come here." His response is "I'll be there in a minute."

Let's see how this would go.

"Tim, please come here."

"I'll be there in a minute."

"That's 1,"

"Oh, all right!"

The reluctant student comes to your assistance.

8. Cross Dialogue

If you have the opportunity to team teach, or if there happens to be another adult in the room when a student or the class is being noncompliant, you can use the technique of cross dialogue.

> **Quick Tip**
>
> With Start behavior tactics, you have some degree of flexibility. You can use one, two, or three strategies on the same problem. You can also switch tactics if one method doesn't appear to be working as well as you'd like.

Here's how it works. Imagine your students are busy chitchatting and will not quiet down. You say to the other adult, "Well, Mrs. Martin, I guess the class is not interested in going to recess today because it is time to line up and they are still chatting." At this point, you should have a few students' attention. Mrs. Martin says, "I agree, Mr. Smith. It is a beautiful day. If the class could just be quiet, I could ask them to line up." Now you have a few more students behaving and elbowing their neighbors while encouraging them to be quiet. You and Mrs. Martin keep doing what you need to do and wait. In a few moments, the class is quiet and ready to go, and you have not raised your voice or given a direction. What an energy saver! The responsibility is on the children, not you.

Simple Requests Revisited

Now let's turn to a question about simple requests. What if, in spite of the fact that your voice quality was matter-of-fact, your request was not spur-of-the-moment, and your phrasing was not wishy-washy, the child still does not comply with what you ask him to do? After reading this chapter, you should now see that you have several options.

For example, Keisha comes in and puts her backpack next to her desk. You have let her know time and time again that all backpacks are to be hung at the back of the room. It is time to break into groups to do different activities, and Keisha starts off for the writing center without hanging up her backpack.

Here are some choices you have at this point:

1. Set the timer for five minutes and tell her, "I want your backpack hung up before the timer goes off." Avoid what we call "shouldy" thinking—the kind of thinking that expects kids to act like adults. If you were into shouldy thinking, you might have said, "I want your backpack hung up before the timer goes off. I already told you that. What does it take to get you to listen to me for once?"

   You could also add a reward or a consequence to the program. You would not do this every time, but sometimes a strategy like this can "jump-start" the kids into remembering a new behavior. "If you do such-and-such before the timer goes off, you can have five more minutes of computer time. If you don't beat the timer, you have five minutes less on the computer." Simple, calm, and straightforward.

2. Could you use the docking system with Keisha's backpack? Yes. If she refuses to do as you ask, you might simply say, "Do you want to hang it up, or do you want to pay me to do it?" Good maneuver.

3. How about natural consequences for this situation? No. This tactic does not really fit here because Keisha likes having the backpack at her desk.

4. Finally, you could consider using counting. Since this is an activity that would take less than two minutes, it would be appropriate. So as the girl is walking over to the writing center, you simply say, "That's 1." She probably won't know right away what you're talking about, so she'll respond with, "What?" Her comment may even be a little ornery.

   That's good—make her think a little. You pause, then say, "Backpack." If she takes care of it in a huff, fine. You probably don't have to count the huff. However, if she yells at you, "WHY DO I ALWAYS HAVE TO DO THAT? IT'S MY BACKPACK! YOU CAN'T TELL ME WHAT TO DO WITH IT!" Pop quiz: What should you do now? You got it! You say, "That's 2," for testing tactic 2, temper.

That's our list of Start behavior strategies. You'll probably be able to come up with several more of your own after a while. Many teachers, for example, have designed different versions of a monthly class party as a form of positive reinforcement for the whole class having achieved a certain well-defined goal, such as fewer than five time-outs for the four-week period. Other teachers send positive notes home or make positive phone calls to parents. What will your favorite Start behavior tactics be?

Getting Started: Rehearsing Your Routines

These are some of the tactics you can use to help set up your routines with your students. The better a routine, the less aggravation and the less motivation is required when the kids have to produce the required behavior. The sign of a good routine is that your prompting and nagging are minimal, and your comments mostly involve positive reinforcement.

It's a good idea to practice the routines once you've defined them. Simply defining a routine and then expecting the students to comply without any rehearsals is the Little Adult Assumption at work in your brain again. Kids need to see, feel, and remember how the particular routine works. So make time for some dress rehearsals of your Start behavior routines—before the procedure actually needs to be used.

With the little ones (under five years old), you can use a model-and-pretend method for practicing. You say something like this: "Let's practice getting ready to go to lunch. Isn't that silly? It's only nine o'clock in the morning! What do we have to do to get ready?" Then reinforce the kids' positive answers.

Next, you describe the process as you model the procedure for them. "First, I'm going to clear off my desk—just like you said. Then

I'm going to get my lunch from the table. Now we line up by the door and wait quietly."

After you've modeled the routine, have the children do it and praise them as they go along. "That's it—you've remembered what was next. Good work." Remember, some kids like business and some syrup!

With older kids (five and up), you can skip the modeling and just ask them to go through the motions. Praise the kids and suggest modifications in what they are doing as necessary.

Once you've rehearsed your routines and started using them, try to keep pretty much to the same time, same place, same way. But what if the kids get sloppy with their lunchtime or cleanup routine? Remember Start behavior tactic 5—natural consequences? A natural consequence of getting sloppy with a routine is needing to rehearse and practice the routine again! No righteous indignation, nagging, or arguing from you is necessary. Be nice and praise cooperation. You'll find that other things will fall back into place.

That's our list of Start behavior strategies. You'll probably be able to come up with several of your own after a while. Next we'll take a look at how to apply these tactics to some of the most common Start behavior problems. You're going to be an expert motivator in no time!

CHAPTER SUMMARY
Your Start Behavior Tactics

1. Praise or positive reinforcement
2. Simple requests
3. Kitchen timers
4. The docking system
5. Natural consequences
6. Charting
7. A variation of counting
8. Cross dialogue

Keep your thinking cap on—and good luck!

14

USING 1-2-3 MAGIC WHEN YOUR CLASS IS ON THE MOVE

How to Handle Your Students When You're Outside of Your Classroom

CONSISTENCY IS A CRITICAL component of effective discipline. Fortunately, once 1-2-3 Magic is up and running, the procedures are fairly easy to maintain. All parties involved know what to expect and, therefore, activities go smoothly. What happens, however, when you leave the safe cocoon of your own room? You now have some added considerations. What if the whole school sees a student of yours acting out at an assembly? What do you do when there is no time-out area? What if you start counting a student in front of the principal and she looks at you like, "Is that all you are going to do?" These pressures can cause you to regress, reverting back to using the Little Adult Assumption and getting caught in the Talk-Persuade-Argue-Yell-Hit syndrome.

Luckily, there are ways to use 1-2-3 Magic no matter what situation you find yourself in. As you use the technique, you will also figure out your own adaptations. In order to be successful in using 1-2-3 Magic outside of your classroom, you need to practice for these other situations with your students before they happen. This advance role-play will be worth its weight in gold—both to you and your kids—when the real crunch time comes.

Keep in mind that there are schools that use 1-2-3 Magic throughout the entire building. This way, all staff members are using the same language with the students. It doesn't matter if the student is getting off the bus, studying in the library, or waiting in the office; any adult can count him if he is misbehaving. One way to introduce this to other staff is to mention it at a staff meeting and show some parts of the 1-2-3 Magic video. Another way is to start using it and when others see how effective it is, your colleagues may ask you to explain it to them.

> **Quick Tip**
>
> Many schools use 1-2-3 Magic throughout the entire building. This way all staff members are using the same language with the students. It doesn't matter if the child is on the bus, in the library, or in the office; any adult can count misbehavior.

Sometimes the principal will ask teachers to try the technique. If other folks in the school are using 1-2-3 Magic, it makes your job a lot easier, and it is easier for the students to understand. The kids don't have to struggle to remember what to do in homeroom vs. music vs. gym. If they are counted, they know they need to shape up or face the consequences. Even if you are the only teacher using 1-2-3 Magic, it is important to talk to your principal, other teachers, and specialists about it, because it may affect the participation of your students in certain situations. These situations are discussed in this chapter.

In the Hallways

Teachers walking in the hallways often have their whole class with them in line. When problems occur, they may need to address the behavior of everyone, or perhaps just the behavior of one or two students.

Let's talk about the whole class first. Initially, you want to meet with your class and talk about expectations for walking in the hallway. *It is also important to practice walking the hall with your class.* This exercise can be done up and down the hall right outside of your classroom, and it does not have to take a long time. You want your students to know what the "right way" looks like and feels like so they can replicate the procedure when the time comes. The children also need to know what the consequences are for reaching a count of 3 so they will not be surprised.

The obvious question then is, "What happens when I get to 3?" There is no handy time-out area in the hall. What you do depends on whether you are counting the whole class or just one student. It also depends on how close you are to your destination. If the whole class reaches a count of 3 in line (because they are all talking, for example) and you are less than halfway to your destination, turn the line around and

Quick Tip

If the whole class reaches a count of 3 in line and you are less than halfway to your destination, turn the line around and go back to the classroom.

go back to the classroom. Once in the classroom, have the students put their heads down for five minutes to serve the time-out.

What if you are on the way to art and the art teacher is waiting for your class? Hopefully, you will have discussed 1-2-3 Magic with all of the specialists (art, music, and P.E.) to let them know that your students may be late if they have to serve a time-out. The art teacher should not change her plan to accommodate the late students. If they only get to do half of their projects, so be it!

Since it is unlikely that every single student was talking in line, you could send a few well-behaving students to art to explain that the rest of the students are taking a time-out and will join them shortly. This rewards the students who were doing the right thing and informs the art teacher of what is happening.

Once the time-out is over, the procedure is the same as after any other time-out. The slate is wiped clean and the class lines up to go to art. It is important that you follow the No Talking and No Emotion rules here. It is tempting to remind the class what they did wrong and that they are late for art or to tell the art teacher all about the miscreants in your class once you arrive at the art room. Don't give in to this temptation.

The above scenario talked about what happens if you are still relatively close to your own classroom. What if you are past the halfway mark, the class reaches a count of 3, and it would not make sense to return to the classroom? If you have discussed 1-2-3 Magic with the art teacher ahead of time, you can let her know that the class needs a heads-down time-out for five minutes. Since you are administering the consequence, you need to stay in the art room for those five minutes. Once the time-out is over, the students get a fresh start and you can leave them in the art teacher's capable hands.

What if only one or two students are acting up? If only a few students are acting up in line, it would not be appropriate to have the whole class take a time-out. In this case, you have a couple of choices. The students could serve the time-out once you reach the destination. For example, if you were on your way to P.E. when the students reached 3, they could sit outside the gym with you for five minutes to serve the time.

Here's another option: if one student is misbehaving in line and reaches a count of 3, she could be required to hold your hand for the rest of the trip, and this would serve as her time-out. This consequence would be especially appropriate for a student who keeps getting out of line or one who slows down the rest of the group by stopping every five feet or so to tie her shoes or look at a bulletin board. With this idea, though, make sure you consider the age and personality of the child. For some students, holding the teacher's hand might be more of a reward than a deterrent.

> **Quick Tip**
> You will certainly want to praise your class and certain individuals when the trip down the hallways goes well.

Speaking of rewards, you will certainly want to praise your class and certain individuals when the trip down the hallway goes well. Some teachers have classroom incentives, and the whole class works together over a month or so to earn something that they all can enjoy.

Now that we've addressed the process of going somewhere with your class, let's look at the discipline at the different possible destinations.

Field Trips

As with the other situations we've just discussed, a well-conceived, preventive approach can make all the difference where field trips are concerned. You need to think about the expectations for your students and a plan for any student who reaches a count of 3. If you have concerns about a particular student, he might even need to earn the trip with positive behavior ahead of time. Check with your administrator to see if this is allowed.

Another thought is to consider having a problematic student's parent act as a chaperone. Preparation for the trip and advance communication with both chaperones and students needs to take place as well. You may want to meet with the chaperones ahead of time or send a letter to them. Prepare your students for the field trip: if they are younger (K–3), you would want to talk with them the day of the trip; if they are older, you should give them the lay of the land the day before.

When you are thinking about your expectations, you need to consider the environment you will be entering with your class. How long will it take to get there? Are you going to be outside or inside? Is it a tour of a factory, an art museum, a zoo, or an interactive play? How many other people will be there? All of these factors go into deciding what to count and what not to count.

Frequently, teachers count less often on field trips because there are lots of activities and distractions. A student may run for a short distance at the zoo and then stop to wait for his friends. You might count running in your classroom, but it would be overkill to do this on the field trip. Think carefully before you count, and ask yourself, "Do I really need to count this, or will it take care of itself?" Often the adult in charge of the group (e.g., the firefighter at the station) will address the misbehavior for you. Not to bruise your ego, but your students might be more likely to listen to a new adult!

Since there is no specific time-out area on the field trip, you need to decide the consequence for reaching 3 and explain this to the boys and girls ahead of time. A teacher, for example, might tell a student to stop and sit on a count of 3. The rest of the group continues the tour while the teacher waits with the student while he serves the time-out. You may want to shorten the time-out to three minutes, although you don't need to share this plan with the student. Also, the other adults need to know what you are doing so they can cover the rest of the group during your absence.

> **Quick Tip**
> Teachers usually count less often on field trips because there are lots of activities and distractions. You might count running, in your classroom, but it would be overkill to do this on a field trip. Do you really need to count, or will the problem take care of itself?

In severe cases of misbehavior, you may need to go to a backup plan in which a student is not permitted to remain a part of the group. Your options include having him wait with an adult on the bus or calling his parents. Make sure you have the emergency information for each child with you; this is typically standard procedure anyway.

Assemblies

Have you ever missed half of an assembly because you were trying to get a student to behave? A disruptive student can be very distracting to the audience during a concert or puppet show. The 1-2-3 Magic program can be helpful at these times. As with all 1-2-3 situations outside of the classroom, you need to think ahead and prepare your students.

One of the best features of counting is that it can be done quietly. Your fingers can do the talking and you do not have to say a thing. Luckily, students who are fooling around frequently check to see if their teacher is watching. When the troublemaker looks at you, simply hold up one finger. You can throw in the "teacher look" for good measure, if you'd like, but you don't have to say, "That's 1."

Continue this method just as you would in your classroom. Perhaps the child decides to shape up; in that case a "thumbs up" and a smile the next time you catch his eye would be a good idea. However, if the child reaches a count of 3, you and the child need to know what will happen. One tactic is to beckon the child with a "come here" finger (still no talking), and he is required

Key Concept

One of the best features of counting is that it can be done quietly.

to sit next to you for the rest of the time period. It would be very distracting to have children moving back and forth after five-minute time-outs during a play or concert. If it is too disorderly to have a student move next to you, another tactic is to have a delayed time-out that the student "owes" you when you return to the classroom or during a preferred activity later in the day. Still another tactic is to "fine" the student using the token economy system we discussed earlier.

In the situations mentioned above, you need to use your professional judgment. Don't worry if you try something new and it backfires—just learn from it and chalk it up to experience. The student's behavior should be the student's problem. This is hard to remember when all eyes are on you and your colleagues are wondering, "What will she do to get him to stop?" Under this pressure, it is easy to slip into old habits. You will be much happier, however, if you stick to the 1-2-3 Magic program! You may even impress a few people by your calm, no-nonsense approach.

Playground

The less structured times of the day often end up with students in trouble and teachers frustrated. How many times has recess concluded with students arguing or someone ending up in tears? There are several factors that contribute to the playground difficulties. First, there is a lot of space, so students can move out of the teacher's line of sight at times. Second, there are frequently multiple classes that include different age groups. There are also large numbers of students present, and some students act like bullies on the playground. Finally, students are often energetic and may impulsively take actions they regret later.

For these reasons, many teachers dread recess. What can you do to keep your sanity during these times, discourage bullying, and try to see that everyone has a good time? Here are several ideas that will help to create a recess period that is less stressful.

Caution

Unfortunately, recess is not a break for you. Though it's tempting to catch up on the latest news from a colleague, a critical factor at recess time is *teacher involvement*. It is important to circulate and to be aware of what your students are doing.

One critical factor at recess is the *level of teacher involvement*. Unfortunately, recess is not a break for you. Teachers must circulate and remain "tuned in" to what their students are doing. It is tempting to take this time to catch up with a colleague or take a breather. However, the more you are aware of what your students are doing, the better. Therefore, it is important to move around. If you stay in one place, it will be easier for your students to disguise or hide what they are doing. If you are circulating, on the other hand, you can use the 1-2-3 program quickly before an innocent remark turns into a full-blown fight.

Another important factor that contributes to success on the playground is praising students for making good choices. As we have just seen, positive reinforcement is an effective method for encouraging desirable behavior. Make sure you direct some of these comments to students who are not right next to you. Upbeat and reinforcing remarks directed to kids who are a ways off let everyone out there know (or at least think) that you are watching everything!

One of your most important playground discipline tools, of course, will be counting. In order to maximize the effectiveness of the 1-2-3 program at recess, you need to give it some thought ahead of time. You need to decide what the countable offenses will be and explain these to your students. Countable offenses that may occur at recess might include:

▸ Fighting (physical)
▸ Yelling
▸ Complaining
▸ Bullying (name calling or physical harassment)
▸ Showing disrespect

> **Quick Tip**
> One of your most important playground discipline tools, of course, will be counting.

Let's look at some of these possibilities.

Fighting

Example: You see two students engaged in a wrestling match. What should you do? First, move close to the students but not close enough to put yourself at risk. Second, say both students' names loudly and say, "Stop. Move away. That's 3. Time-out." Notice that you would go straight to 3 for fighting. There are no warnings due to the serious nature of the offense. This would have been explained to students and practiced during the original 1-2-3 Magic orientation.

Next, indicate the time-out area for each student. The students should not be close to each other. If you did not see the cause of the fight, both students should receive equal consequences.

Remember the Little Adult Assumption and the No Talking and No Emotion rules while you are making this intervention. Resist the urge to ask, "Who started this?" That question will inevitably get you two students pointing at each other and no fair way to determine the cause of the conflict. Therefore, treat them both as equal contributors. They were both fighting when you saw them; consequently, they both receive five-minute (or longer for more serious incidents) time-outs. It may also be helpful, at another time, to meet with these students to discuss their interactions and role-play some different problem-solving techniques with them. Another important consideration is that many schools have a school-wide policy about fighting. Depending on the seriousness of the fight, you may also want to consider parental involvement.

Yelling, Complaining, Bullying, and Disrespect

When actions such as yelling, complaining, bullying, and disrespect are involved, it will often be the case that only one student is counted and the basic 1-2-3 procedure will be followed. Where will the time-out area be? It can either be next to you or—if you are moving around a lot—next to a building, fence, or another identifiable area that you can watch.

If you repeatedly observe one student bullying others, this student should, of course, be counted with each incident. In addition, this problem should be discussed as soon as possible with the special services team, with the bully, and with that student's parents. On the other hand, if you repeatedly observe one student being bullied by others, the bullies should all be immediately counted (automatic 3s are usually appropriate), special services should be involved, and the appropriate parents contacted (including the victim's).

Should loss of recess be used as a disciplinary consequence? One question that frequently comes up in discussions of recess is, "Can I keep a student out of recess for misbehavior earlier in the day?" A problem with this notion is that students frequently need recess in order to burn off energy, and losing this opportunity early on may contribute to more problems later in the day.

> **Caution**
>
> Using the loss of recess is a possible option, but consider other alternatives first.

Using the loss of recess is certainly an option, but consider these questions. First, would a more immediate consequence work better? For example, if a student is disrupting a lesson, he may not later connect the delayed consequence of missing recess to his earlier disruption of the lesson. Perhaps a time-out, token fine, or other alternative would be more effective. Second, would it work if the consequence were the partial loss of recess time? The student might serve a five-minute time-out next to you at the beginning of recess, for example, then be allowed to go and play afterward. Remember to check whether loss of recess time is allowed in your school district.

Lunchtime

Most teachers these days do not eat lunch with their students. There may be a rotating list of staff members who serve "lunch duty," or there may be an adult who is the regular lunch monitor. Regardless of the system in your school, it is possible that you could get a bad report about one or more of your students on a given day from whomever is monitoring the lunchroom.

What do you do about this? It would not make good sense to give the kids time-out so long after the fact, and you were not there to see what happened anyway. The only options for using 1-2-3 Magic at lunch are these: (1) you are there with your class and use the 1-2-3 the same way you do in the classroom; or (2) the lunch monitor learns the technique and uses it with the students. In either case, when using 1-2-3 at lunch, there needs to be an established time-out area in the cafeteria. Since lunch periods are pretty short, it may make sense for the child to stay in time-out for the remainder of the lunch period. And since separation from the group—not hunger—is our primary goal, the student should be allowed to eat his lunch while in time-out.

CHAPTER SUMMARY

In order to be successful in using 1-2-3 Magic outside of your classroom, you need to practice for these other situations with your students before they happen. This advance role-play will be worth its weight in gold—both to you and your kids—when the real crunch time comes.

15

COORDINATING ARRIVAL, DISMISSAL, AND TRANSITIONS

Time-Saving Tips for Moving between Activities

THERE ARE CERTAIN TIMES of the day when Start behavior tactics are especially important. Those times include arrival, dismissal, and transitions. At these times teachers find themselves trying to get their students to hang up backpacks, put finished work in the right place, clean up, and clear their desks. When arrival, dismissal, and transitions go well, you save time—and don't all teachers want more time?

Arrival

Before your students arrive, you should already have your materials and lesson plans ready so you can stand at the door to greet the children. This daily welcome goes a long way toward establishing positive relationships with your students. By greeting your students, you are sending the message that they are important to you, while at the same time modeling organization and preparedness.

A vital component of having a calm and structured arrival time is routine. A sample routine, for example, might be:

1. Greet the teacher
2. Turn in homework
3. Hang up backpack and coat
4. Start working in journal

To establish a routine, the necessary procedures must not only be discussed with the class, they must also be practiced. Since kids are just kids, and because they are not naturally neat, orderly, and efficient, rehearsal of routines is of tremendous value in helping the kids master classroom procedures. In fact, some teachers occasionally use rehearsal as a kind of natural consequence. One year, just two days before winter vacation, for example, one teacher observed that her third grade class had just gone through their most noisy and chaotic arrival of the entire year. Without any angry lecturing, this teacher had all her students put their coats back on, pick up their backpacks, and go line up in the hall. She then had them reenter the classroom in a calm and orderly fashion. Twice.

> **Quick Tip**
>
> An example of a good sample routine to start each day is:
> 1. Greet the teacher
> 2. Turn in homework
> 3. Hang up backpack and coat
> 4. Start working in journal

Students who follow the routine should be publicly praised. In the pre-vacation example just described, our diligent teacher lavishly praised her kids during both of their orderly reentries.

Have you ever noticed that your students are very chatty in the morning, and it is difficult to get them to settle down? One teacher accidentally found a great way to get her class to be quieter in the morning. The teacher had laryngitis and could not speak above a whisper. She found that when she spoke in a whisper, so did her students. So she had an idea. She trained her students to whisper for the first fifteen minutes of the day. She found that the students were much calmer during arrival time, and they could actually hear the morning announcements when they came over the loudspeaker. What a relief!

Dismissal

Dismissal can be a stressful time of day. Notes need to be sent home, everyone must have the items they need for homework, announcements are being made, questions are being asked, and everyone (especially the teacher) is tired. Again, routine is important here. Students need to be trained on what to do at the end of the day: pack up, clear desks, and so on. The teacher may need to speak to individual students or to write notes to parents, so she needs to find an activity all students can do while she accomplishes these tasks. Some teachers have students silently read for the last twenty to thirty minutes of the day. This activity gives the teacher some freedom, and it also provides time for kids to practice an important academic skill in a calm, quiet manner.

Other teachers prefer to read aloud to students as the pupils pack up. Of course you would pick a book that is very interesting so students are quiet in order to listen. This method works well with older students who can pack up on their own while listening to the story.

The way students are dismissed varies from school to school, and you'll need to figure out what kind of dismissal strategies work best within your school environment. We recommend having students wait until all final announcements about buses and so on are made, then wrapping up your day in the classroom with a clear signal that it's time for students to leave. Using the same phrase, such as "Have a wonderful afternoon," or "See you tomorrow, class!" can be a good way to indicate to your students that the day is finished and they are free to go.

Transitions

We often hear that students have difficulty with transitions. If changing from one activity to another takes a long time, precious academic time is lost. We have been in classrooms where teachers stand in front of the class for five minutes saying over and over, "Class, take out your math book and turn to page 52." "What page?" "Page 52. Boys and girls, let's go, we have a lot to cover today. Jeanie, you need your math book, not your social studies book. Samantha, put the crayons away. Come on everyone…math book…page 52, please." What an exhausting process!

One Start behavior tactic that works really well during transitions is positive reinforcement. Generally, when you announce to the class that they should get out their math books and turn to page 52, you will have a few immediate compliers. Make sure you compliment those folks by saying, "I like the way Matt followed my direction. I see that June is on page 52…good for you! Thank you for getting your math book, Jovaughn." As you do this, you will notice a phenomenon occurring. Other students will start doing what you want them to do.

As we often say, "You get more of what you pay attention to." This positive reinforcement strategy is much more constructive than focusing on the students who are not doing what you want. Recognizing students who are following directions well by saying something like, "I see Valerie is ready because her book is open to the correct page" will motivate the others to follow suit.

In addition to transitioning between subjects, classes must transition

> **Key Concepts**
>
> One Start behavior tactic that works well during transitions is positive reinforcement. Make sure you compliment those who are following directions.

to other locations throughout the building, which requires lining up. This is another activity that can take an inordinate amount of time. With younger students, music can signal transitions such as cleaning up or lining up. With older students, you can turn the procedure into a "game." As students answer a question successfully, they can line up quietly. This is also a nice way to multitask. Not only are the students lining up, they are also reviewing the curriculum. The same tactic described earlier can also be used here. Students who are behaving well can be the first to get into line. Remember to compliment the student so the others know why you picked her. For example, "I see that Kim is quiet and her desk is clear. Kim, please line up. Let's see, is anyone else ready?"

Let's test your creative abilities at this point. Can you think of ways that you might use a kitchen timer in your classroom to help your students transition quickly and smoothly? Many teachers have!

By the way, just because you feel a time crunch during transition times, don't forget your counting procedure. Don't have time for a time-out because someone has to catch a bus? Use your time-out alternatives.

Teachers are constantly saying, "I need more time!" Using the Start behavior tactics to get students to come in and get to work or get ready to leave the classroom is one way to save a lot of time during the day.

CHAPTER SUMMARY

1. Establish daily routines for arrival, dismissal, and transitions.
2. Rehearse as needed.

16

COMPLETING CLASSROOM JOBS AND CHORES

Tactics for Getting Your Students to Clean Up after Themselves

DIFFERENT TEACHERS HAVE DIFFERENT amounts of tolerance for the level of orderliness in their classrooms. Some teachers have piles of papers on their desk that may look messy to other people, yet these individuals can find what they need in a matter of moments. Some teachers have the same messy-looking situation, but these people cannot find what they want without a good deal of time and trouble. Other teachers have precise color-coded filing systems that are tucked away so their desks remain totally free of clutter.

It's easy to imagine that teachers with such different styles might hold quite different expectations for how orderly they want their students to be. Whatever your personal preference is, however, we recommend some semblance of order so you and your students can focus on the tasks at hand: teaching and learning! That's why classroom jobs and cleanup are important.

With that in mind, we need to remember that kids are not naturally neat. Many—if not most—are more naturally messy. The conclusion? The children will have to be trained to clean up. How can you accomplish that? By this time you shouldn't have to be reminded that you won't get the kids to complete this unpleasant chore by nagging or delivering the lecture "The Seven Reasons Why It's Easier on Me if You Pick Up after Yourselves."

Instead, you have several options for cleanup. If you use your innovative ability, you can probably come up with several more. Here are some good ones.

Expectations

First and foremost, it should be an expectation that students complete their assigned classroom jobs, keep their desks neat, and pick up after themselves. As always, you need to keep the age of the student in mind as you determine the appropriate strategies to use. Most students take pride in doing their unique classroom jobs, such as line leader, messenger, and so on, so these tasks typically are not problem areas. It's the nonunique, routine tasks where the kids may need a little more motivational help from you. If you have a student who becomes argumentative about doing an expected task, you would count the arguing. Later, you may need to conference with this student and make up a contract or a chart.

> **Quick Tip**
>
> It should be an expectation that students complete their assigned classroom jobs.

Music

Music can be helpful during any cleanup. When younger students are cleaning up from indoor recess, for example, the teacher can sing or play a cleanup song to remind her little ones that it is time to put the toys away. When the song is over, all children should have cleaned up and returned to their spaces. Teachers of older students may play music between subjects to signal that it is time to put one activity away and get out the materials for the next subject. All of this should be practiced ahead of time so the students know what to do.

Kitchen Timer

Another helpful cleanup device is the kitchen timer. Sometimes you need the boys and girls in your class to clean up quickly. At such times, the teacher should get the attention of the class and say, "OK, guys, I am challenging you to beat the clock. When I say, 'Go,' you have seven minutes to put everything away and return to your desks. Let's see who can beat the clock…Go!"

There are also times when a timer is needed for a particular student. If one child is constantly taking a long time to clean up, you can use the above "Race the Clock" technique with her. It may be that she also needs a five-minute warning before it is time to clean up because some youngsters are more upset about having to stop an activity than they are about having to clean up afterward.

Fines

Of course, there may be times when a student flat-out refuses to clean up and has already taken a time-out for the refusal, and now it is the end of the day. Unless you are able to keep the student after class that day, you will probably be cleaning up for the student. What the student needs to know is that this "service" is not free. You are going to use a version of the docking system. If you have a token economy system, you can

> **Quick Tip**
>
> If you have to clean up for an obstinate student, use a version of the docking system. The child can pay you back tokens if you have a token economy system, or he can "owe" you some of his free time.

fine the student. If not, he could owe you some of his free time. The point is that you want the student to learn that it is faster and "cheaper" to pick up after himself rather than having you do it for him.

Competition

A variation on using the "Beat the Timer" technique is the "Who Can Clean Up Fastest" technique. Individual students could try to win, or the competition might be between table groups. For this approach, you can also build in bonus points if needed. Each student or each table group can have a piece of masking tape on which the teacher can note a tick mark for each bonus point. The bonus points can be the reward or can count toward artificial reinforcers.

Random Positive Reinforcers

One teacher used a visit from the "Desk Fairy" as a random reinforcer. Every once in a while the Desk Fairy would come to visit the class after school. The children who had neat, clean desks found a glittery note and a piece of candy on their desks. This provided ongoing motivation for students to keep their desks clean because no one knew when the Desk Fairy would come.

CHAPTER SUMMARY

Tips for Jobs and Cleanup:

1. Expectations
2. Music
3. Kitchen timer
4. Fines
5. Competition
6. Random positive reinforcers

17

GETTING THE
SCHOOLWORK DONE

How to Keep Kids Focused and On Track

KIDS' MAIN JOBS IN school are to work and learn. This means doing their own schoolwork and not bothering their classmates. An effective classroom teacher helps her students accomplish these two goals by organizing the school day, actively engaging the children in learning, and monitoring their performance and progress. She also has a discipline plan, such as the one found here in *1-2-3 Magic in the Classroom*, that is consistent and effective in both preventing behavioral problems as well as dealing with them when they inevitably arise.

In this chapter we'll take a look at how both effective teaching and effective discipline help to get the work and learning done. Let's imagine two fourth-grade students, Brandon and Whitney. Neither child is officially diagnosed with attention-deficit/hyperactivity disorder (ADHD), but they are both definitely spirited and often challenging. We're going to try to imagine how the very first hour of their day at school might go if they were faced by teachers with two of our theoretical teaching styles: detached and authoritative.

Brandon and Mr. Hanson

Spirited Student: Brandon
Detached Style: Mr. Hanson

8:30 A.M.
Brandon enters the classroom with his usual high level of energy. Mr. Hanson looks up from grading papers at his desk with some degree of uneasiness. He remembers, just two weeks ago, when Brandon was absent with the flu for three days. How easy the class had been to manage for that short time! Mr. Hanson sees Brandon as a potential aggravation—not as a challenge.

8:32 A.M.
Out of the corner of his eye, Mr. Hanson watches Brandon as other kids enter the room. "What will be his first stunt today?" the teacher wonders. Sure enough, instead of hanging up his backpack, getting his homework out of it, and starting to work on his journal, Brandon drops the backpack on the floor and starts teasing the girl—who is writing in her journal—who sits on his left. After several minutes of this, Mr. Hanson feels he needs to intervene.

8:34 A.M.
"Brandon, what are you supposed to be doing?"
   "I don't know," Brandon replies defensively.
   "Get to work on your journal, please. Now."
   Brandon slowly gets his journal out of his desk.

8:38 A.M.
After trying to write for four minutes, Brandon starts looking out the window as if he is trying to find something more interesting to

occupy his attention. Mr. Hanson glares at him. Brandon sees the look and picks up his pencil again.

8:42 A.M.
Brandon starts talking to the boy who sits to his right, asking the other student what he is writing and stating that journal writing is stupid. Mr. Hanson overhears part of the conversation and ignores it in spite of his growing irritation. Why can't this kid cooperate for a change? The teacher doesn't think it's worthwhile reprimanding Brandon again since he never responds to correction and because in three minutes the class will make the transition to math anyway.

8:45 A.M.
Mr. Hanson announces the transition to math. "OK, class, please get out your math books and turn to page 78." Brandon takes his math book out of his backpack, then takes this opportunity to get out of his seat for the purpose of hanging up his bag on the wall. Mr. Hanson, however, wants the transition to math to be quick.

"Brandon, what are you doing?"

"I'm hanging up my backpack."

"That should have been done when you walked in the door this morning."

"I forgot."

"Well, I'm getting a little tired of your 'forgetting.' Put the backpack down and return to your seat immediately."

The irritated boy tosses the backpack, then moves slowly back to his seat. Mr. Hanson tries to ignore the lad while he gets the rest of the class started with math. "OK, kids, I'd like you to solve the first three problems on page 78. When you're done, raise your hand." Mr. Hanson returns to his desk to grade some more papers. The math problems should take most of the kids four to five minutes.

8:48 A.M.
Brandon raises his hand after getting back to his seat. "Which problems are we supposed to be doing?" he asks.

"Brandon," Mr. Hanson says, his irritation now closer to the boiling point, "you seem to be having a lot of trouble getting organized this morning. If you don't know what problems to work on, it's because you weren't paying any attention before. Now get to work!"

Brandon asks the boy next to him what problems they are supposed to be doing. Mr. Hanson finally blows up.

"I did not ask you to talk to your neighbor. I asked you to simply do your work."

"But I don't know what to do."

8:50 A.M.

Brandon is written up and referred to the assistant principal. Mr. Hanson's note refers to three misbehaviors: not following directions, talking out of turn, and disrupting class.

How Did Mr. Hanson Do?

In less than one hour, Brandon—who is certainly no angel—has been referred for office discipline. But part of the problem was Mr. Hanson's detached teaching style. This teacher's classwork organization and structure were weak, and he made little attempt to positively engage Brandon in the desired academic tasks. Mr. Hanson did, however, monitor Brandon, but the monitoring was done with the often-fatal "I'll wait and see what kind of trouble he gets himself into and then react" approach. Mr. Hanson's reactions, finally, were just that: reactions. First a look, then an angry reprimand or two (accompanied by too much little-adult type talking), then an office referral.

Mr. Hanson's Summary List
Little attempt to positively engage
Monitoring was done with fatal "I'll wait and see" approach
Interventions were reactions
Too much adult talking
Office referral

Whitney and Ms. Roberts

Spirited Student: Whitney
Authoritative Style: Ms. Roberts

Let's redo this first hour of the morning in another classroom right down the hall. Here Ms. Roberts will be dealing with Whitney, a nine-year-old girl whose behavior and temperament are almost identical to Brandon's. Note how Ms. Roberts does a better job of providing structure, engagement, and monitoring, and also note how her discipline plan fits nicely into her academic operations. Though she is not always successful, Ms. Roberts does her best to see Whitney's behavior as a challenge—not as an aggravation.

> ### Quick Tip
> Though she is not always successful, Ms. Roberts tries to see Whitney as a challenge, not as a potential aggravation. This point of view helps this teacher prevent problems through structure, engagement, and monitoring. But she also keeps the 1-2-3 procedure ready for immediate use.

8:30 A.M.
Whitney enters the classroom with her usual high level of energy. Ms. Roberts greets her at the door, along with her classmates. "Whitney, good to see you. That dog of yours didn't run away again last night, did he?"

"No way," says Whitney.

"Now tell me, young lady, what is that big word on the board for?" On the blackboard the word *JOURNAL* is written in huge letters.

"I got it, I got it," says Whitney.

8:32 A.M.
While circulating through the room and greeting other students, Ms. Roberts watches Whitney as other kids enter the room. The girl hangs up her backpack, gets her homework out, and puts it on Ms. Robert's desk, and then returns to her table. Whitney starts to get her journal out, but her teacher knows that this pupil of hers doesn't like to write and she is easily distracted. The girl writes for a couple of minutes.

8:34 A.M.

Whitney starts becoming interested in the neighbor to her left, who is diligently journaling. Feeling a little jealous, Whitney asks, "What's so interesting that you need to write about?" When the other girl doesn't respond, Whitney taps her pencil on the table and says, "Hey, you."

Ms. Roberts knows from past experience that Whitney won't persist with a writing assignment without fairly frequent interventions. She sees the girl getting off task and talking, so the teacher tries to help reengage her in her work with some next-door praise. "It's good to see children like Michael *(to Whitney's right)* working hard on their journals. Good job, kids." Whitney takes the hint and starts writing again.

8:38 A.M.

After trying to write for four minutes, Whitney starts looking out the window as if she is trying to find something more interesting to occupy her attention. Ms. Roberts focuses her gaze on the girl and smiles with an encouraging glance. Whitney sees the look and picks up her pencil again.

8:42 A.M.

Whitney starts talking to Michael, asking the other student what he is writing and stating that journal writing is stupid. Ms. Roberts overhears part of the conversation and is prepared for this next minor challenge. "Whitney, that's 1." Nothing else is said. Whitney knows very well what a count means, and she stops talking and returns to work.

8:45 A.M.

Ms. Roberts announces the transition to math. "OK, class, please get out your math books and turn to page 78." Whitney takes her math book out of her desk. Ms. Roberts wants the transition to math to be quick and painless. Standing in front of the class, she says "It looks like Dale has his book out, and Whitney is also on page 78 already, and so is Karen. You kids are doing this in record time! Whitney, can you read the first problem for us?"

Whitney proudly reads. This is something she is good at. The rest of the math lesson goes smoothly.

9:05 A.M.

Ms. Roberts is pleased with the morning so far. "OK, kids, you've done such a good job today, I'm giving you five minutes of free time. You may draw, read, rest, or whisper to your neighbor, but remain at your desk. We'll be going to music shortly, and I want you all to remember our routine for walking in the hallways." As she walks around the room giving these instructions, Ms. Roberts passes by several children's seats. She gives them all—including Whitney—a quick pat on the shoulder.

How Did Mrs. Roberts Do?

Getting the work done is no easy job when you have twenty-five kids to keep an eye on. Effective teaching means actively organizing the day, engaging students in the learning process, and monitoring their work and behavior. Effective instruction also means having a clear and consistent discipline plan.

Mrs. Roberts's Summary List

Positively engages student immediately

Monitors in friendly manner

Interventions proactive and constructive

Little unnecessary chatter

Happy ending

18

CONDUCTING CLASS MEETINGS

How to Make Your Classroom (Almost) a Democracy

THE CLASS MEETING IS an opportunity to work out school-related issues that come up on a regular basis. The point of the meeting is to involve the students in solving problems. If the teacher always solves the problems and makes the decisions, how will the students learn to do this? Problem solving and getting along with others are two skills that students need to learn now so they can be responsible citizens later. To some of our boys and girls, this problem-solving orientation seems to come naturally; to others it seems to be a foreign concept. The class meeting provides an opportunity for all students to learn about this process by being involved.

Basic Principles

The class meeting is just what the name implies. In an organized fashion, everyone in the room discusses problems that have come up lately. The meeting time can also be used to exchange positive feedback and compliments. Class meetings probably will not work with preschoolers and kindergartners, but students in first grade and beyond can usually make good use of this time. The class meeting should be held weekly, although special meetings can be called as needed.

There are a few additional reasons why the class meeting is a good idea. We have already discussed the benefits of children learning problem-solving skills. It's also good for children to get used to contributing their own opinions and to listening to other people share their ideas. In addition, kids will often cooperate better with a decision or policy when they have had a say in the development of that idea.

> **Quick Tip**
> Students in first grade and beyond can usually make good use of class meeting time.

How to Run the Class Meeting

The format of the class meeting is very simple, and the guidelines we'll present here are only one of many possible ways you can conduct yours. With younger pupils, the teacher is the chairperson and has the responsibility for keeping order and for keeping people on task. Older children can have a try at running the meeting themselves from time to time if you think they can handle the job well enough. In some classes, a class president is elected, while in others the position rotates throughout the group. The chairperson sees to it that the agenda is followed and that each person gets a chance to speak without being interrupted.

What is the agenda? It's very simple. Anyone who has a problem related to the class can bring it up at the meeting. Some teachers set up a system in which the students submit topics ahead of time to avoid having too many items on the agenda or personal items on the agenda. Also, sometimes the issue may go beyond the scope of the classroom. In this case, the administrator may be invited to the meeting. With each issue, the chairperson guides the group through each stage of the meeting.

Steps for Classroom Meetings

1. The person who submitted the item describes the problem she wants resolved.
2. Other pupils give their thoughts and feelings about that problem.
3. The floor is opened to proposals for solutions; anyone can speak, but one at a time.
4. A solution to be tried is agreed upon. This final idea may combine aspects of the suggestions from different people. If there are disagreements, the teacher has the final say.
5. The agreed-upon solution is written down on a piece of paper that is then posted on a bulletin board. The solution can also be written in a class meeting journal or notebook or entered in a computer.
6. The next person brings up his problem, and steps 2–5 are repeated.

Most solutions are considered experimental in the beginning, especially if the plan is complex and differences of opinion about it are many. If the proposed resolution doesn't work too well, that idea can always be reviewed at the next meeting. Although proposals should be concrete, specific, and practical, don't be afraid to make them flexible and imaginative!

Sitting through these class meetings is not always easy. If you're hoping these will be warm, fuzzy experiences, that may not be the case. In fact, class meetings can be downright difficult to manage at times, so it's a good idea to keep them relatively short. Many adults agree that this type of meeting is simultaneously one of the most aggravating and one of the most effective things you can do with your students. If you can get through the process, people do have a greater tendency to follow through with the agreed-upon solutions. It's also nice that everyone has a chance to speak out and to learn some negotiation skills.

Typical Issues That Can Be Discussed at Classroom Meetings

1. Bullying
2. Lunchtime problems
3. Monthly class rewards
4. Possible field trips
5. Respecting property
6. Sharing

What if students bring up issues such as shortening the school day, longer summer vacation, or the belief that there is too much homework? Let the kids know in advance that there are certain issues that are not negotiable because school is not a total democracy.

Caution
Classroom meetings can be very effective, but sometimes aggravating!

Social Skills

Many teachers like to incorporate some type of character education into their class meetings. One teacher in particular took the class meeting to another level by creating a "Friendship Society." One year she had a multiage class of first- and second-graders. Several of the students in the class started their own club. Eventually, however, the students who were left out began to feel rejected, while the students in the club adopted certain negative behaviors to "fit in" with this select group.

The teacher, consequently, took the opportunity to start her own club called the Friendship Society. All students were members of the club. There was a "secret" handshake and membership cards for all to enjoy. Instead of the typical class meeting, there were meetings of the Friendship Society. At the beginning of the meeting, the teacher highlighted a positive social skill such as shaking hands or apologizing. She would read a book, perform a puppet show, play a video, or teach the students a new behavior having to do with friendship.

After the lesson, students would talk about the ways that they had been friendly that week. They might share, for example, that they lent a friend a book, that they shared a toy, or that they told the truth. Each act of friendship would earn the class a sticker on the Friendship Chart. After the kids counted the number of stickers on the chart, the teacher would ask if there were any troubles needing the attention of the group, or she would bring up a problem that she had noticed. At this point the meeting took on the look and feel of the class meeting. By the end of the year, the students not only had Friendship Society T-shirts and membership cards, they also had created a caring community in the classroom and learned some new interpersonal skills they could take with them.

CHAPTER SUMMARY

The class meeting may not always be an easy activity to endure, but it does provide a good opportunity to:

1. Teach problem-solving skills
2. Teach social skills
3. Teach negotiation skills

19

DISCUSSING BEHAVIOR ISSUES WITH YOUR STUDENTS

Strategies for Choosing the Right Time to Talk and What to Say

THE NO TALKING AND No Emotion rules do not mean that you should never talk to kids about their troublesome behavior. But there are good times to talk and explain, and bad times to talk and explain. Generally, the time when a rule is being enforced is a bad time. Why? There are several reasons. First of all, this brief period of time when you are enforcing a rule is not a good learning moment for most kids. You are likely to be irritated, and chances are the student is mad at you, too. He or she may at the same time feel anxious, guilty, and defensive about what just happened.

Second, talking during this time of unpleasant emotional arousal encourages arguing. There are lots of children who do not relish the idea of humiliating themselves in front of all their classmates by admitting that you—and all your reasons—are correct, while their behavior was absolutely wrong. To save face, therefore, the youngsters may feel obligated to disagree with you. If you get into an argument over what just happened, you have accomplished nothing.

Third, it is very likely that all your ideas about the child's behavior are correct. Adults are not stupid, and they do not go around saying dumb things to children most of the time. Even though your ideas are good, the child is not open-minded during discipline episodes. At that moment she doesn't want to hear what you have to say, and your attempts to explain only aggravate her more. This irritation motivates your pupil to contradict what you are saying— even if only in her mind. So what have you accomplished? You have given the little one an opportunity to throw your good ideas into the trash.

Finally, talking when a rule is being enforced will break up the flow of your classroom instruction or routine.

When should you talk about problems? You should explain something right away if a child's problem behavior is new, unusual, or dangerous. If a child swears in your presence and this behavior is new and unusual, you would explain to the child why he can't do that. Remember to keep your explanations short and to the point. Look at the child's facial expressions; you can usually tell when he is tuning you out, so make your point and wrap up the conversation.

Key Concept

The time when a rule is being enforced is a bad time to talk and explain rules, unless the issue involved is new, unusual, or dangerous. Better times to explain are after praising someone for following a rule or during class meetings and one-on-one conferences.

Many teachers find that a good time to explain a rule is right after praising a student or the whole class for following that rule. "You kids got your books out right away during that transition. That makes my job a lot easier, and it saves us a lot of time."

Another time to talk may be during a class meeting, as we have just explained. And finally, there may be times when you choose to speak individually to one of your pupils.

One-on-One Conferences

There may be times when a one-on-one meeting with one of your students is in order. This may be the case when there is a chronic or serious problem that needs to be discussed. You may be thinking to yourself, "Well, I wish I had time to do that." Our response is that you need to make time early on for these conversations before the situation becomes a big problem taking up a lot of your time in a negative way. Meeting with a student one-on-one is a proactive approach that will save you time in the long run. How do you make the meeting work?

Your choices for meeting times with a student are obviously before school, during the school day, or after school. When you choose to meet with a student depends on the situation itself (Do you need to handle it right away or can it wait?) and the amount of time you need (Is this a five-minute conversation or a fifteen-minute one?). If you are going to meet with the student before or after school, you will need to enlist the help of the parents in making sure that the student has transportation. Some schools have before- or after-school programs in which students are involved, so the students are there early or late anyway. You may want to meet with the student at these times in order to be able to focus 100 percent of your attention on the conversation.

When you meet with a student during the day, however, you have the rest of your class to think about. What will the other students do when you are having your meeting? There are many options for how and when to meet with your students.

Options for Meeting with Students during the Day

1. Having lunch with the student.
2. Talking with him on the playground before he joins his friends.
3. Meeting at library time, when other students are involved in picking out books and another adult can monitor them.
4. Meeting when other students are working independently on an assignment. (Make sure the student with whom you are meeting will have time to finish the assignment later.)

After you decide that a meeting with a student is warranted, you must do a couple of things. First, you need to decide on your goal for the meeting. Second, you need to inform the student of the meeting. Do you want to have a dialogue with the student to find out what she is thinking or what might be causing her behavior? Do you want to explain something to the student? If you know the purpose of the meeting, it will be easier to stay on track and take care of the issue at hand rather than becoming sidetracked.

Letting the student know that you need to meet with her can be done verbally or in writing (if the student is able to read). Sometimes students can become anxious about the meeting and might ask, "Why? What did I do?" Just let them know that you will discuss the matter at the scheduled time rather than responding to their question directly. This way you will not get caught into having a discussion before you are ready.

Ask a Few Questions First

Instead of jumping in and anxiously explaining right away, when time permits, many adults use a kind of questioning technique to help kids think a problem through. During a class meeting or one-on-one conference, for example, you might ask questions like these:

> What would happen if you did that?
> Why is this a good thing to do?
> How did you feel when I said that to you?
> Why do you think I want you to do your work?
> Why is it a bad idea to push someone?
> Why do I ask you to be quiet?

Questioning forces children to think issues through themselves, rather than passively listening to your lecture—however brilliant it may be. This important mental activity, in the presence of a non-angry adult, often helps kids remember the lesson a little better. Questions followed by brief adult explanations can be an effective strategy for teaching children how to behave. Whether you decide at any one point to explain or to question, keep in mind that short, calm talking sessions are always better than long, angry lectures.

Don't Forget How Children Learn

In spite of your explanations, a girl in your second-grade class still whines occasionally when she doesn't get her way, and she often forgets to clean up after herself. When she whines, you have told her to use her "big-girl voice." When she leaves toys and books lying around, you have explained that there will be consequences.

Remind yourself not to be too hard on her. It takes children a while to learn how to avoid Stop behavior and how to successfully complete certain Start behaviors. So give your youngsters a break—be patient and realistic.

Adults often forget that children's mastery of behavioral skills depends not only on insight (explanation) but also on practice (repetition). You certainly didn't master the art of driving a car by simply reading about it in a book. You also did not become a competent driver simply because your driving instructor told you where the ignition, steering wheel, gas pedal, and brake pedal were. Although those concepts were useful bits of knowledge, you still had to go out and practice, practice, practice. And you had to practice under different conditions. You had to drive in good and bad weather, with a pleasant or angry or worried adult, and sometimes you were in a good mood, sometimes in a bad mood.

Quick Tip

You did not learn how to drive a car by reading a book. It took practice, practice, practice. Don't ever underestimate how much behavioral rehearsal is required for children to master skills like talking in a normal voice, cleaning up, remembering to turn in homework, and being considerate of others.

The same is true of children. Don't ever underestimate how much behavioral rehearsal is required before kids can master skills such as talking in a normal voice (when frustrated) and remembering to clean up (when it's almost time to catch the bus).

If you want to give your students a little talk from time to time about good and bad behavior, by all means do so. But try not to talk right at the time a rule is being enforced. And keep in mind that kids are not little adults; you don't train them to behave just by pouring information into their heads. In addition to our explanations, we adults often forget that our youngsters have many other ways of learning good and bad behavior:

- Modeling by adults
- Modeling by other children, including classmates and siblings
- Books, television, and music
- Praise that follows good behavior
- Counting that follows undesirable behavior
- Adults' comments regarding the behavior of other people
- Behavioral experimentation: trying out something and seeing what happens

When discipline or conflict is not involved, of course, talking is less of a liability and more of an asset. It is through talking that a lot of learning takes place. In fact, one of the things most teachers love about kids is the opportunity to observe these young minds think, grow, learn, and change. Small children are learning machines, and it's fascinating to be a part of—and to encourage—that learning process.

CHAPTER SUMMARY

Think it over before you deliver a long lecture on good behavior. You don't want to disrupt your classroom instruction and routine. Better times to talk or explain might include:

1. During a class meeting
2. During a one-on-one conference
3. Right after praising a student

PART V

Strengthening Your Relationships with Your Students

Classroom Discipline Step 3

CHAPTER 20
Utilizing Praise, Fun, and Forgiveness

CHAPTER 21
How to Practice Sympathetic Listening

CHAPTER 22
Working Collaboratively with Parents

20

UTILIZING PRAISE, FUN, AND FORGIVENESS

How to Start Each Day with a Clean Slate

WE PUT PRAISE, FUN, and forgiveness in the same chapter because they are intertwined. Praise is a self-esteem builder because it recognizes and reinforces competent behavior in a child. When students are doing what you want them to do, it is easier to have fun with them. Yes, schoolwork and learning can be fun! Forgiveness is necessary when children make poor choices that aggravate us. It is important that we forgive them so their mistake does not cloud our future interactions.

When it comes to praise, fun, and forgiveness, however, teachers have a harder job than you might expect. While these three activities are obvious self-esteem boosts to children, as well as great relationship strengtheners, adults usually do not engage in these types of behaviors nearly as often as they should. We mentioned one reason for this deficit in chapter 13: the "angry people make noise; happy people keep quiet" tendency. This "rule" refers to the tendency of adults to give feedback to children when the adults are angry, but to keep quiet when the adults are happy with the children's behavior.

Our inherent psychological inclination to speak more when angry—and to not praise or act affectionately unless we really, really feel like it—is one of the big reasons why we asked you first to learn how to control students' undesirable behavior in step 1, and later to learn how to encourage kids' positive behavior in step 2. Success at steps 1 and 2 will make you more inclined to consistently apply the relationship-strengthening parts of the 1-2-3 Magic program. Your success with those two initial tasks will automatically make you feel more encouraging toward your kids and also make you feel more like giving them positive feedback. That extra motivation is very important because you are human, you are busy, and you can't always remember to do everything you're supposed to do.

But a positive feedback deficit can also result from two other things: (1) how a teacher is feeling about life in general and (2) how that teacher is feeling toward a particular child, in general and at any one particular moment. Just because a child does something that is commendable, for example, does not mean that he or she will be recognized or praised for that action. Let's examine these two issues.

How Are You Doing?

Research has confirmed what common sense has long suggested: adults who are unhappy and suffering in their own lives are not going to give a lot of praise to others. Depressed adults, for example, are known for being somewhat removed, isolated, and at times almost indifferent to those around them. These folks simply do not have a lot of extra positive energy to pass around. And children in their presence know it and feel it. These are some of the possible reasons for the detached teaching style we described in chapter 5.

Anyone's energy can be sapped by long hours in a stressful job that involves issues such as a difficult supervisor, poor clerical support, and impossible challenges. In addition, lots of energy can go into worrying about personal issues. Stressors like these can make adults more self-centered and less likely to appreciate and reward kids for the good things the little ones do.

The moral of the story is that to effectively express praise, have fun, and exercise forgiveness in your classroom, you must take good care of yourself. You need to see that your needs are being met personally.

Whatever the case, how you handle your students will depend, in large part, on your success in diagnosing and resolving your own problems.

> **Quick Tip**
>
> To praise your students frequently, have fun with them, and forgive them when they make mistakes, you need to see that your life, your needs, and your problems are being taken care of. Don't kid yourself: you are not a superhero.

Your Feelings toward Your Students

We have seen teachers over the years who have been extremely upset over the behavior of one or two students who are disrupting the whole class. The tendency is then to blame the child or the parents: If only the student would try harder or listen. If only the parents would feed him breakfast and get him to school on time. Then things would be better.

When teachers take on this outlook, it externalizes the problem in a way that is not constructive. The real bottom line is that teachers need to do the best they can for their students during the school day. There are so many other factors that educators are not able to control. Of course, if there is a serious situation at home, such as suspected abuse, you must report it through the proper channels right away. But otherwise teachers must make the most of what they *can do* rather than worrying about what they can't do.

In order to make the most of the time that teachers have with their students, they need to separate the child as a person from the child's behavior. We have all heard the phrase, "I love you, but I just don't like you right now." Let's take that a step further and change the message to "I like you, but I don't like what you are doing," or "I like you, and I also like what you are doing."

Teachers say that students will tell them things like, "I am a wild man. You are not going to like me." Where did these kids get these ideas? Adults have told them that in the past. In order to help students turn themselves around, teachers have to help their pupils realize that they have the power to make good and bad choices, but their choices do not make them good or bad people.

This is where the concept of forgiveness comes in. True forgiveness does not mean that you have to agree with or condone what a child has done. The message can be, "What you did was not OK, you paid the consequence, and now we can move forward." The key to forgiveness here is that the adult truly does move forward. Holding on to a student's mistake until "the next time" can sabotage the idea of forgiveness.

Key Concept

True forgiveness does not mean that you have to agree with or condone what a child has done.

Imagine a student calls you a name. She would, of course, be immediately counted to 3 and would have to take a time-out. After five minutes, she comes out of time-out, and of her own volition, she apologizes sincerely. You say that she is forgiven and you move on. Wonderful.

The next day, however, the same thing happens: she calls you a name again. You launch into a Little Adult lecture: "Well, that is the second time this week, young lady. You said you were sorry, but I guess you didn't mean it. I can't believe we're going through this again. When are you going to realize that I am here to help you? I will not be treated this way!"

Was the student truly forgiven the day before? No. If the forgiveness had been sincere, the slate would have been clean. In this case, the girl's past transgression was thrown back in her face as soon as the teacher had the opportunity. This is not the way to build trust.

Every day, teachers have the difficult job of letting go of both major and minor resentments. How can this be accomplished? The answer, in large part, is to follow our three discipline steps. First, you work hard at reasonably and calmly counting the kids so they don't drive you crazy with their talking, whining, running in the halls, or showing disrespect. Then you have to put on your thinking cap and establish your routines for Start behavior so these kids don't further aggravate you by being late to class, messing up the classroom, or not getting their work done. And finally, you need to pay attention to all the simple but effective relationship-building strategies we're discussing in Part V of this book, which include praise, fun, forgiveness, and sympathetic listening.

Be patient with yourself and your class. Habits are hard to change. If you keep working at the three steps, you will find that you like your students more. You'll also notice that they like you better and they also listen more often, which leads to your praising them more frequently.

In many ways, praise, fun, and forgiveness are to kids what water and fertilizer are to plants. You probably went into teaching because you love kids. Sometimes a difficult situation can make you forget this important historical fact. Working on your relationship with your students—while continuing to get the work done—can help you get back in touch with the original motivation for your career choice.

CHAPTER SUMMARY

Regular Doses of Praise

+

Shared Fun

+

Regular Doses of Forgiveness

=

Good Relationships

21

HOW TO PRACTICE SYMPATHETIC LISTENING

Why It's Important to Hear What Your Students Have to Say

YOUR THIRD-GRADE STUDENT, TOM, storms back into your classroom after lunch. You don't know what happened, but Tom is still visibly upset. Though this boy is normally a good student, you fear his emotional turmoil will interfere with his work during the afternoon. You can't count him because his being angry is no crime, and the incident is over. You also don't want to interrupt your math lesson, which will start in just a few minutes, nor do you feel it is right for Tom to talk about his feelings in front of the whole class.

Here is a time for an attempt at what is often called "sympathetic listening." You call Tom over to your desk, and sympathetically ask:

Teacher: "What happened?"

Tom: "Debby took the last brownie at lunch and she knew I wanted it!"

Teacher: "How did she know that?"

Tom: "I was talking about it on the bus."

Teacher: "That must have made you very upset."

Tom: "I'm going to show her!"

Teacher: "Boy, I haven't seen you this mad for a while! So what happened after she took it?"

Tom: "She held it up and made faces at me! It was bad enough that she took it; I can't believe she made me look so stupid in front of everyone else!"

Teacher: "So she not only took the brownie, she also made fun of you?"

Tom: "Yeah. Why does she do stuff like that? One minute she's nice and the next minute, she's a total jerk."

Teacher: "Well, after all that, are you going to be up for math?"

Tom: "Yeah, I guess."

Sympathetic Listening and Self-Esteem

Sympathetic listening is a way of talking to someone with empathy. Sympathetic listening is very respectful of another person's thoughts and feelings because the listener doesn't just sit there, but instead attempts (the "active" part) to see the world through the other person's eyes.

When you are actively listening to a student, you are setting aside your own opinions, suspending judgment, and committing yourself to completely understanding how the child saw a particular situation (you don't have to agree with him). In our example, the teacher is not thinking that her student caused the trouble. Nor is she formulating her own response.

> **Key Concept**
>
> A sympathetic listener tries to see the world or an incident from another person's point of view. This approach takes patience and self-restraint, and it requires that you communicate back to the person talking what you think he is saying.

Sympathetic listening, therefore, tries to accomplish two things: (1) to understand what another person is saying and thinking—from his or her point of view—and (2) to communicate back and check the understanding with the person doing the talking. The listener is an active participant in the conversation, not someone who just sits and nods from time to time (although sometimes that's not so bad either).

Sympathetic listening is not always easy for adults. It takes time and requires that you keep your opinions to yourself. Once you get past the point of feeling artificial or too passive, though, you can sometimes pleasantly knock the kids right off their feet with this tactic. And listening is an excellent way to begin any more lengthy, serious conversation, such as you might have during a class meeting or in a one-on-one conversation with one of your kids.

How Do You Practice Sympathetic Listening?

First, get yourself in the proper frame of mind: "I'm going to hear this kid out—even if it kills me—and find out exactly what he thinks." Next, several different approaches can be used, and once you get used to them, the whole process should feel very natural.

Strategies for Sympathetic Listening

OPENERS

You often start the listening process with what are called "openers"— brief comments or questions designed to elicit further information from your student. These comments often require self-control, and they are especially difficult when you are caught off guard by an emotional issue. Openers may also appear incredibly passive to you, but remember that sympathetic listening often needs to precede any problem-solving discussion. This is especially true, for example, when dealing with upset parents.

Openers can be very simple, such as "Oh," "Wow," "Yeah," or "What." An opener can be anything that communicates that you are ready and willing to listen sympathetically, including nonverbal behavior, such as sitting down next to the student or putting down your papers to look at him. In the previous example, the teacher's opener was, "What happened?"

NONJUDGMENTAL QUESTIONS

After openers, it's often necessary to ask questions to further your understanding of what a youngster is talking about. To be effective, these questions must not be loaded or judgmental. "Why did you do a stupid thing like that?", "What's your problem today?", or "Why are you bugging me now about this?" are not good questions. These comments simply express irritation from the listener, and they will likely receive an argumentative or silent response.

Here are some better questions that keep the talk going and further understanding: "What do you think made you do that?" or "What was going through your mind at the time?" In our earlier example, the teacher asked, "So what happened after she took it?" That was a good question.

REFLECTING FEELINGS

A third sympathetic listening strategy is called "reflecting feelings." If you are going to tell someone that you think you understand him, try to let him know that you can imagine how he must have felt under the circumstances. Sometimes when you reflect feelings, older kids will tell you that you sound a bit like a psychiatrist. If that's the case, just say, "Sorry, but I'm just trying to make sure I understand what you're talking about."

In the example, the teacher reflected feelings back at two points: "That must have made you very upset," and "Boy, I haven't seen you this mad for a while!" Other examples of reflecting feelings might include "You really sound bummed out about that," "That must have really been fun," or "You were pretty upset with me."

Reflecting feelings accomplishes several things. First, it lets the child know that whatever he is feeling is OK (it's what he may do about it that can be right or wrong). Second, the reflecting response reinforces self-esteem. And third, reflecting feelings also helps diffuse negative emotions so they are not acted out somewhere else.

PERCEPTION CHECKS

From time to time during a talk, it is helpful to check out whether you are really getting a good idea of what your youngster is saying. Perception checks also tell a child that you're really listening and really trying to see the world through his eyes for a moment.

Examples of perception checks or summaries might be: "Sounds like you're saying that I am not being fair to you," "You felt it was your worst day at school this year," or "You wish you could spend more time reading for pleasure?" In the earlier example, the teacher's summary was this: "So she not only took the brownie, she also made fun of you?" That was a nice, sympathetic comment.

Sympathetic listening is a communication skill, but it is also an attitude. We are talking about your attitude, not your student's. It's the attitude of sincerely trying to figure out what someone else is thinking, even if you don't agree. This, of course, is a different kind of job if you're talking to a two-year-old instead of a ten-year-old. Either way, it's a great self-esteem builder for children. You'll also find that if you listen well, you learn a lot about what children think about life.

> **Quick Tip**
>
> Sympathetic listening is an attitude. You're a good active listener if you are really trying to understand what the other person is saying. You're a bad active listener if you're preparing your rebuttal while the other person is talking.

Sympathetic Listening and Counting

Sympathetic listening helps you to understand your children, and listening also helps to diffuse negative emotions. That's fine, but if you practiced sympathetic listening all the time, you wouldn't be any kind of a disciplinarian. You also might not have time to finish all your lesson plans for the day. Sympathetic listening, by itself, has nothing to do with setting limits and enforcing rules. Imagine this scene:

Frank: "Hey, lady, why did I get an F? I studied really hard for this test!"

Teacher: "You're feeling pretty frustrated right now."

This teacher's response is overly nice. It is also inappropriate. The child's disrespect is way out of proportion to the situation and should be addressed by counting.

On the other hand, if you counted all the time whenever the kids were upset, you wouldn't be a very understanding adult. Your class would correctly perceive you as only an instrument of discipline—or worse. Imagine this scenario:

Amanda: "I'm bored."

Teacher: "That's 1."

That's a pretty insensitive and unnecessary response. Your boys and girls certainly won't want to talk to you very often! So how in the world is a teacher supposed to know when to listen and when to count? One consideration involves time and the other consideration involves the issue the child is upset about. Sometimes this decision is easy, but often it's not. Here are some guidelines.

Time

Taking time to listen to a child will do a lot for your relationship with that student. As adults, we know that it is frustrating to bring up a meaningful topic to a friend or family member, only to have them half-listen while watching TV or stop listening to take a phone call. One of the best ways to let someone know that they matter is to stop and really listen.

But do you have the time right now to listen to a child? A teacher's day is very busy, and there are certain learning-related tasks that have to get done. As mentioned earlier in this chapter, sympathetic listening is an appropriate technique to use at scheduled times, such as in one-on-one conferences and class meetings.

In general, though, much of your sympathetic listening is going to happen in bits and pieces throughout the day. Many times, students just want someone to briefly hear them out and, once that has happened, they will go on with their day. In such cases, it may be sufficient to listen to what the student has to say and provide a comment such as, "I'm sorry to hear that you are feeling down. I hope things get better," or "Thank you for telling me your good news. You seem really happy about that." These types of responses will be enough to satisfy some students.

In other situations, though, you may not be able to take the time the student needs right at that moment. If you find yourself in this position, you will need to let the child know that you want to hear what he has to say, but it will have to happen at a later time. You may say something such as, "I can sense that what you have to tell me is important. I want to talk with you at lunch so I can give you my full attention. Right now, we are late and need to get going."

If the issue is not an "emergency," another alternative is to ask the child to write you a letter or a journal entry about the subject. There are several benefits to using this option. First, the student can really think about what she has to say and its importance. Second, you can take the time to read her thoughts and decide the best response (writing back or talking with the student). Third, the student is practicing her writing skills. And fourth, you have documentation of the student's concerns.

If you do not have time to listen to something a student has to say, and you don't think it can wait, you may want to see if the counselor, an administrator, or another teacher that the student knows has a moment to spend with the child. One teacher prepared notes ahead of time on colored paper that said, "Mrs. Smith, this child really needs to talk something out. If you have a few minutes, please listen to what he has to say and then send him back to class." The teacher set up this arrangement with Mrs. Smith ahead of time. In cases that needed immediate attention, the teacher simply handed the student the colored note to deliver to the designated adult. When the student was upset, sometimes the walk down the hall to deliver the note was enough of a break to help the student calm down.

How to Apply Sympathetic Listening and Counting

Here are some examples of how you might accomplish the sometimes tricky job of sympathetic listening and counting.

Issue I: The Child Is Not Upset with You

If the time is appropriate, and if the child is upset about something that didn't have anything to do with you, it is probably time to actively listen. This behavior couldn't be testing and manipulation directed at you because you didn't do anything to frustrate the child.

You're out at recess, for example, and seven-year-old David comes running up to you, yelling.

"THOSE GUYS ARE JERKS!"

"Who's that, David?"

"The kids on the slide—they won't let me have a turn."

"Why not?"

"I don't know. They're just morons."

"Boy, you sound really upset!"

"Yeah, I'm not playing with those creeps."

"That sounds like a good idea."

The teacher doesn't count the yelling. The problem occurred outside of the teacher's earshot and didn't have anything to do with her. Unless she concludes that David is being bullied on a regular basis, this adult figures a little sympathetic listening may diffuse the situation.

Or, back to the boredom routine with Amanda:

"I'm bored."

"You're not having a very good day, huh?"

"No. I don't like indoor recess on rainy days."

"You try, but you can't think of anything fun at all?"

"Nope. Can I go get that book from the library that I wanted?"

"You know, I need to send a note to the librarian anyway. Why don't you take this note and get your book at the same time?"

"All right!"

Here the teacher doesn't get trapped into making seven suggestions that will be shot down one by one. Her pupil is not feeling so good, but this isn't badgering or any other type of manipulation. It's time for a little sympathetic listening. If the two can work out something to do, fine. If not, see the next example.

Issue II: The Child's Upset Switches to You

Sometimes the kids will start out upset by something else, but then their frustration will switch to the teacher. In that case, try sympathetic listening, but you had better be ready to count.

Amanda's situation above is a little tricky. What if the teacher doesn't think it's possible for her to go to the library?

"I'm bored."

"You're not having a very good day, huh?"

"No. I don't like indoor recess on rainy days."

"You try, but you can't think of anything fun at all?"

"Nope. Can I go get that book from the library that I wanted?"

"I am afraid not."

"Aw, why not?"

"That will take too long, and I don't want to send a buddy with you who's enjoying their recess."

"Samantha will go with me."

"Look, why don't you join Samantha at the computer? You two could play that game together."

"If I have time to do that, why can't I get my book?"

"That's 1."

"Oh brother." *(Amanda walks away.)*

Here the teacher tries sympathetic listening, but it doesn't diffuse the situation. Amanda tries to put the burden on the teacher's shoulders. The teacher can't give Amanda what she wants, so Amanda gets into testing—badgering, martyrdom, and a little intimidation. The teacher catches herself getting verbally involved in the dead-end discussion and starts counting.

Discuss Problems, Count Attacks

What if the kids are upset with you in the first place? This situation gets even trickier. It depends partly upon how the little ones approach you. In general the rule is "Discuss Problems, Count Attacks." "Hey lady, why did I get an F? I studied really hard for this test!" is an attack from the start.

Some children's comments are not quite attacks, and if an adult uses a little sympathetic listening, the emotion may be diffused. Let's say you are monitoring a student in detention. The following scenario might occur:

"Why are you making me do this stupid math worksheet now!?"

"Math's not your favorite subject, is it?"

"Whatever." *(Child starts his work with a sigh.)*

Here, the sympathetic listening helped diffuse the unpleasant emotion, so the child didn't act on it. Keep the 1-2-3 program ready in your back pocket, though, because you may not always be so lucky:

"Why are you making me do this stupid math worksheet now!?"

"Math's not your favorite subject, is it?"

"Yeah, I hate it!"

"Boy, you really don't like it, do you?"

"I could be home watching TV right now."

"You'd really prefer to be at home relaxing."

"DON'T JUST SAY BACK EVERYTHING I SAY!"

"That's 1."

The responses in this example show remarkable presence of mind on the part of this adult.

CHAPTER SUMMARY

Sympathetic listening is a great self-esteem builder and a good way to help kids think through problems—when you have the time for it! Remember to use:

Openers
Nonjudgmental questions
Reflecting feelings
Perception checks

22

WORKING COLLABORATIVELY WITH PARENTS

How to Get Parents Invested in Their Child's Behavior at School

TEACHERS HAVE USED THE 1-2-3 program successfully in the classroom for many years. In fact, in many preschool and elementary schools, 1-2-3 Magic is the basic discipline system for the entire school. We have found that many parents become interested in 1-2-3 Magic once they see it working successfully at school. Some schools using the 1-2-3 process in the classroom have also trained many of their parents to adopt the method. This coordination is nice for the children because they then have the same system in both places. The consistency makes it easier for them to respond appropriately. Like their parents and teachers, children are happier when there is less hassling about discipline.

Whether counting is being used at home or not, the communication between home and school is a main ingredient in school success for each youngster.

1-2-3 Program at School Only

In the cases where 1-2-3 Magic is being used only at school, it is a good idea to let the parents know that you are using it. If you are starting 1-2-3 Magic at the beginning of the school year, send a letter home to the parents describing the procedure. Here is a sample letter you might consider.

Sample Letter to Send to Parents:

DEAR PARENTS AND FAMILIES,

I am very pleased to be your child's teacher this year, and I look forward to getting to know you and your child over the next few months. I would like to take this opportunity to let you know about a discipline program that will be used in my classroom this year. Dr. Thomas Phelan, a clinical psychologist, developed this program, called 1-2-3 Magic: Effective Discipline for Children 2–12. It is a program that incorporates specific, gentle techniques to stop undesirable behavior as well as to encourage positive behavior.

Of course, the number one priority during the school day is instruction. I want your child and all of the students in the class to learn as much as possible this year. I find that by having a discipline program that is both warm and demanding, my students and I are able to put the majority of our energy into academics.

Parents and teachers have used 1-2-3 Magic successfully since 1984. This is an evidence-based program that is easy to use and that works very effectively.

There are three steps to 1-2-3 Magic:

Step 1 involves managing undesirable behavior by counting to 1, 2, or 3. On the count of 3, the student must take a five-minute time-out. This simple technique is remarkably helpful, but only if the adult using it follows what are known as the No Talking and No Emotion rules.

Step 2 involves encouraging good behavior. There are several simple methods for encouraging constructive actions in kids, such as across-the-room praise, other forms of positive reinforcement, charting, and timers.

Step 3 involves using some valuable tools for maintaining healthy relationships with children, including sympathetic listening, shared fun, and class meetings.

All of these steps work together and contribute to a positive classroom climate where your child will feel welcome and comfortable, and where he or she will work and learn productively.

I will be sharing more information about 1-2-3 Magic on Back-to-School Night, which will be held on _____. In the meantime, please let me know if you have any questions. I can be reached at _____.

Sincerely,
Your Name

1-2-3 Magic at Home and at School

With some of your students, there may come a time when you'll want to suggest or encourage the parents to use 1-2-3 Magic at home in addition to your using it in the classroom. Remember that many of these parents will already be somewhat familiar with the program because of the letter you sent home and also because of your Back-to-School Night presentation. The use of 1-2-3 Magic both at home and at school can develop in the following ways: (1) at a parent-teacher conference, a parent mentions having great difficulty managing the child's behavior at home; or (2) you feel the child is still too difficult in the classroom, and home/school consistency might help calm the youngster down.

The critical component of using this discipline program at home and at school is that the adults at home use it the same way that the teacher does. One teacher, for instance, started counting on the first day of school, and a particular student got very upset. When the teacher called home, he found out that the parents were using the 1-2-3 program as well. However, it turned out that the time-outs at home lasted well over an hour. No wonder the little guy was so disturbed! Just because folks say they are using 1-2-3 Magic does not mean that they are doing it correctly.

There are other ways that adults may use counting incorrectly with their children. Some parents count too fast, not allowing five seconds between counts. By far the most common mistake made when using 1-2-3 Magic, however, is talking too much and getting too emotional. When you are talking with family members who claim they are using the 1-2-3 program at home, it is important the teacher be a good listener—be sure to use the sympathetic listening strategies discussed in the previous chapter.

If parents have a "twist" on the 1-2-3 program that works and that is firm, rational, and gentle, that may be fine. If their variation is not working or is too harsh, however, it may be time to employ all of your skills in diplomacy. Teachers cannot tell parents how to raise their kids, but rational adults can talk about what works for the benefit of a child. The adults in each child's life need to be open and willing to compromise in order to do what is in the best interest of the child. When you are using 1-2-3 Magic in the classroom, your biggest selling point for the program in dealing with parents is that it works for their child in your classroom.

CHAPTER SUMMARY

Consider using 1-2-3 Magic both at school and at home when:

1. The child's behavior is still too difficult to manage at home
2. The child's behavior is still too difficult to manage at school

PART VI

Tips for Using 1-2-3 Magic at Different Grade Levels

CHAPTER 23
Preschool and Day Care

CHAPTER 24
Elementary Grades

CHAPTER 25
Middle School

CHAPTER 26
A Note about Students with Special Needs

23

PRESCHOOL AND DAY CARE

Using 1-2-3 Magic with Young Children

MANY ADULTS WONDER HOW children as young as two or three can understand 1-2-3 Magic. Is it really fair or reasonable, for example, to count kids this little? Well, we have news for you: children of preschool age are smarter than we often give them credit for. We may think they do not understand something when really they just want us to think that! Before the age of two, a child not only understands what "No" means, but also uses the word—often.

At two years old, children can understand simple questions (Where is your dog?) and respond to one-part directions (Pick up the toy). At three years old, children are starting to use three-word sentences, follow two-part directions (Put on your coat and get in line), and understand prepositions (Put the cup on the table). At four years old, most children can express basic feelings about themselves and others (I am mad; she is sad).

Based on this information, we know children can follow simple directions given in the classroom at an age as early as two years.

Children can also tell the different tones in your voice along with the different types of facial expressions.

When you ask a child to stop or wait or you say no, most typically developing children should understand the request. If they do not listen, then it is time to implement 1-2-3 Magic. 1-2-3 Magic is very useful in both small and large classrooms with average students as well as children with special needs.

Before Using 1-2-3 Magic

Since young children are just learning how to socialize and handle routines, it may not be necessary to start immediately with the 1-2-3 program (though many schools do). Some preschool or day care teachers also want to avoid singling out a child with the counting process, at least in the beginning. If a child is out of line with his behavior in a group, the teacher's first two alternatives can be:

1. Simple distraction: guide or interest the child in another activity
2. Separation from the group for a short time

Small children are fairly easy to distract, and then the whole problem can be forgotten. If the child needs to be separated from the group, he can sit in a chair or on a spot on a rug for a kind of time-out period. In some preschools, the child is then allowed to determine when he wishes to cooperate and is ready to return to the group. If problems continue, however, the teacher determines when the child will return from subsequent rest periods.

Putting 1-2-3 Magic into Action

Teaching is both an art and a science. Even when we have a "formula" (like 1-2-3 Magic), it is important for teachers to use their judgment regarding implementation and practice. Some preschool students/classes are ready, and some are not. We must look at each individual child as a "whole child"—what are their strengths? What are their areas for growth? Also, what is the class "make up?" More boys than girls? More extroverts than introverts?

In our classrooms, there may be a range in ability of three to four years (or more), depending on the subject. Therefore, in a fourth-grade class, there could be students reading at a second-grade level and students reading at a fifth-grade level (with everything in between). The teacher must differentiate to include and teach at all levels. The same is true with addressing behavior and social skills deficits.

In preschool this challenge is even more pronounced and difficult in some ways because many of the children have never been in a school environment; therefore, they need to learn each skill (how to sit in a chair, how to line up, how to wait, and so on). These are the "learning to learn" behaviors that preschool teachers must teach in addition to colors, shapes, letters, and numbers. And even though a child has a cognitive age of two, he or she may be much more immature emotionally.

Some preschool teachers want/need some time to teach and practice the "learning to learn" behaviors before counting students. If the children do not know what the correct and incorrect behaviors are, we cannot hold them accountable until we teach them and have evidence that they understand. Preschool teachers often look for "gentle" ways to guide, redirect, and teach the student in the moment.

For example, in a class of three-year-olds, if Joe grabs a toy away from Bob on September 10, the teacher may come over and quietly say, "Joe, we need to ask for the toy. Please give me the toy and I'll show you." If the same scenario happens on December 10, she would count Joe for grabbing because he has had time to learn and practice the rule.

To get started with 1-2-3 Magic in your preschool classroom, you need to do a few things. You will first need a time-out chair/area that is only for sitting and waiting to complete the time-out. The area needs to be away from the other children and free from distractions (e.g., no toys within arm's reach).

When starting to count, you can comment on the other children's good behavior while you are counting someone who is not following directions, or you can just start counting. If you do the latter, you need to start at the beginning of the day, and the children need to know and understand there is a consequence if they get to 3.

When counting, it is very important that the child understand that your tone of voice has changed from fun and playful to serious. When using 1-2-3 Magic, say the numbers with conviction. It is true you do not want to do a lot of talking or explaining to the children, but try simple statements like "I am going to start counting. If I get to 3, you are going to time-out, not outside with us." Remember to let the young child know that there is a consequence if he gets to 3. This phrasing needs to be used initially until you know that the children in your class understand that if you start counting, they are going to time-out or will miss out on something the other children in the class get to do.

With preschoolers, we recommend that you use some type of visual cue along with the counting. There are a few things you can do. You can use your fingers along with the words as you are counting and showing 1, 2, and 3. You can have premade visuals (e.g., sad faces) that you can point to each time you say a number so children can see if they get to the third picture, they are going to have to face the consequence.

> **Quick Tip**
>
> With preschoolers, we recommend that you use some type of visual cue along with the counting.

Another idea is to have a large picture (approximately 8 by 10 inches) of the place where the child will have to go for time-out. Take the picture and cut it into three equal parts, then each time you count, add a piece to the picture. When the whole picture of the time-out area is visible (on the count of 3), the child can see that he needs to go to that area.

Praising other children in the class who are behaving properly is another way to help a child learn what she is supposed to do. It also avoids giving her the negative attention she may be looking for from you. For example, if Jenny is sliding the toys off the table and onto the floor, you say, "That's 1, Jenny." Then turn to Chris, who is playing nicely with the cars on the floor and say, "I like the way you are playing with the cars on the ground. Great job driving the car into the garage." This helps Jenny to understand a correct way to play with the cars versus the way she is playing with them. It also gives positive reinforcement to Chris so he will not feel that he needs to act out to get your attention.

Especially with young children, you do not want to sit down and have a long heart-to-heart conversation with them after the time-out. However, you will need to make sure that they understand why they had to go to time-out. This can be a quick "Thank you for sitting nicely. Show me how you play with your friends and keep your hands to yourself." When they show the appropriate behavior, you can praise them, and then they can rejoin the group.

One teacher started the 1–2–3 Magic program in her class by just counting the misbehavior of one child. When that child got to 3, she had him go to the time-out chair. The boy did not stay in the chair for a long time. The purpose of this first run-through was to give all the children an example of what would happen if the teacher counted to 3, and also to let the kids know the teacher was serious. Once the other children observed what happened, they generally started to follow through with requests to stop undesirable behavior before the teacher reached 3.

If this is your first attempt using time-out in a preschool or day care setting, thirty seconds to a minute should be an adequate time to have the child separated from the other students. After the first couple of days, when the children understand there are consequences when you get to 3, you can lengthen the time-outs. The length of the time-out, for example, might depend on the severity of the behavior. Another good rule of thumb for longer time-outs is one minute for each year of the child's age. After the children are used to the system, it is likely you will not be getting to 3 very often.

Quick Tip

Pick a time-out chair or area that will be used only for time-out. This area should be away from other children and free from distractions. When you start counting, make sure your voice changes from playful to serious.

Other Considerations

1-2-3 Magic is a very effective behavior-management tool, but there are times when you need to be aware of other things that could be going on with the child. You need to consider whether a child may be sick, may be sad about something, or may not understand what is expected of her. All three of these situations can lead to children exhibiting poor behavior. Children at this age can be feeling sick and not know how to tell you, or they may feel that something is wrong but not know what it is exactly, so they do not tell you anything at all.

> **Key Concept**
>
> For the first few days of using the 1-2-3 program in your preschool classroom, thirty seconds to one minute of time-out should be adequate to get across the idea. After that, you can lengthen the time-outs. And don't forget to use lots of praise too!

In any of these situations, the following scenario may occur. You see the child doing something he should not be doing, and you start counting. The child, however, gets more upset because he does not feel good for one reason or another; you continue counting, and he ends up in time-out. He may stop the behavior while he is there, but he may still have some issues that you will need to cope with once he is done with time-out. Though it is not usually a good idea to have a discussion with a child right after he comes from time-out, after a few minutes, it might be a good idea to check with the child to see if something may be out of sync for him.

If the child is upset about something, perhaps some sympathetic listening and other forms of emotional support are called for. Kindness, fun, and affection can go a long way in helping a child feel better. But remember to continue to count—gently but firmly—what you have defined as misbehavior in your classroom.

Tantrums

Tantrums from little kids often present adults with uncomfortable situations. Often children feel that they have control when they are throwing a tantrum. Typically, the teacher is looking at them and trying to get them to stop, while other children are also paying attention to the disturbance. Generally the child throwing the tantrum is looking for attention from the caregiver, and sometimes it does not matter whether it is positive or negative attention. Tantrums are usually done for the benefit of an audience.

In order to get a handle on preschool-age tantrums, there are a few key factors to keep in mind. If you can tell that the child is not going to harm himself or others, turn away. Then turn calmly toward the child, say, "That's 1," and then turn back. You can use the previously mentioned 1-2-3 visual aids, if needed, but do so quickly and do not make a big production out of it. Some kids won't look at your visuals anyway during these times.

If the tantrum becomes extreme and other children are becoming disturbed, it might be time to go to the angry child, tell her that she is OK, and then look away. If the child does not start to calm herself down, you can continue counting if you have already started. Another tactic here is to move away from the child and engage the other children in the room in something fun that the tantruming child may like. In this case, you might say, "Lisa, that's 3. After a calm time-out you can join us. Your time will start after you are quiet."

If the tantrum is disturbing other children and none of these measures help, the child will be escorted from the room. He can be led to a room or other unoccupied and confined area with limited distractions, where one or two teachers or staff stay with him until his tantrum is over. As the child is yelling or thrashing around on the floor, one adult periodically tells him, in a calm and reassuring voice, that he has two choices. He can either continue screaming on the floor and stay where he is with the teachers, or he can stop the tantrum and return to the classroom to play with friends. Nothing else is said. Patience is essential!

For the teacher in charge, the most important aspects of managing the little ones' temper tantrums are (1) knowing exactly what you are going to do in advance and (2) remaining calm.

Conclusion

Children in preschool and day care—approximately ages two to five—are at the stage where they need to learn basic socialization skills as well as the ability to follow the instructions involved in a daily routine. Parents want their children in these situations to be able to respect the rights of others, to learn to give and take, and to feel good about themselves. They also want their kids to be able to handle a time period of two hours or more that involves activities such as music, story time, snack time, free play, group sharing time, and arts and crafts.

Good, consistent discipline provides a basis for allowing these kinds of learning to occur. If a class of children—no matter how small— is continually out of control and no one gets along, little learning occurs, and everyone's self-esteem suffers.

CHAPTER SUMMARY

Get your little students off to a great start in their educational careers by using 1-2-3 Magic early. You'll be doing them—and their future teachers—a big favor!

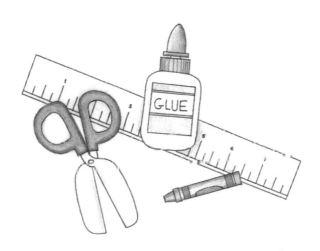

24

ELEMENTARY GRADES

Using 1-2-3 Magic with Grades K-5

IN THE ELEMENTARY GRADES, there is a wide range of skills, abilities, and personalities among the students. Elementary teachers are expected to teach all subjects in addition to playing roles such as nurse, parent, judge, and jury at times. Elementary students in general tend to want to please adults, but as they get older, they enjoy "testing the waters" to see what they can get away with. There is a lot going on in the elementary school environment.

The last thing an elementary school teacher has time for, therefore, is a student who is misbehaving. This is where 1-2-3 Magic comes into play. Elementary school teachers need a quick and easy-to-use procedure to cut down on undesirable student behavior (Stop behavior). They also need something that will help encourage students to do what they need them to do (Start behavior). The beauty of the 1-2-3 approach with elementary students is that the method works well and is easy to implement—even when a teacher is busy or stressed. 1-2-3 Magic is most effective at this age when expectations and consequences are clear and when there are other educational rules and procedures in place to create a structured, positive, and engaging classroom environment.

The New Deal

At the beginning of the elementary grades, students are really learning what it is like to be in school. Even if a child has participated in preschool, the structure is different in elementary school. The day includes more academics and is usually longer than a preschool day. This change is a lot for the students to get used to. In one classroom, for example, one little first grader who had been in half-day kindergarten started packing up her backpack at 12:00. When her teacher asked what she was doing, she said, "It's 12:00. Time to go home." The teacher kindly explained that in first grade, the students stay until 3:15, to which the child replied, "Well, who signed me up for this?" For each year of elementary school, teachers need to help their students adjust to changes such as this.

> **Quick Tip**
>
> When they hit first grade, the kids are really learning what it means to be in school. "All day long" is a lot to get used to. To help orient the newcomers to the 1-2-3 program, some teachers have students from last year's class come in to help demonstrate.

Implementing 1-2-3 Magic in elementary school is similar to implementing it at home. It is important to explain to the students at the beginning of the year how the 1-2-3 program works and then start using it right away. Some teachers have students from last year's class come in to demonstrate the technique. This is good for your current students because they see older students as their role models. We also recommend that you send a letter home to parents or explain the system to them at Back-to-School Night so they will know what it means when their child says, "My teacher counted me."

The 1-2-3 Procedure

When using the 1-2-3 program in an elementary classroom, the teacher says the student's name or makes eye contact when undesirable behavior occurs. Then she states, "That's 1." If the same behavior or an equally serious behavior occurs, "That's 2." If the student does not correct herself, "That's 3, take five." Then the time-out is taken.

Typically, five-minute time-outs work throughout elementary school. Of course, there are always some exceptions, and you can adjust the time according to the maturity level of the child. Some teachers have students watch the minute hand on the clock and have the student rejoin the group after five minutes have passed. Other teachers set a timer with an audible bell to signal the student. There may be occasions when it is advantageous to have a timer that the student can watch. This may be reassuring to students who do not have a firm concept of time and who become anxious that they are "never" going to get out. Watching a timer may also help a student who is upset to calm down. If the student is watching the timer, it is important to set up rules surrounding the timer so it is not misused. If the student cannot handle the responsibility of having the timer, it returns to the teacher.

Most students will comply with this system and shape up after a count of 1 or 2. However, a few students may reach 3 a few times per day, especially in the beginning. For these students, you may need to build in consequences for multiple time-outs. Remember: the goal is to have students monitoring their own behavior and correcting themselves, so we want to help them reduce the number of time-outs per day. This doesn't mean that if a student goes to time-out, the system isn't working; you just need to keep the big picture in mind.

The trap that elementary school teachers most frequently fall into is too much talking. Students this age are inquisitive and, during academic time, you want them to be. So teachers are used to talking and explaining things to their students all day long. The 1-2-3 program should be the exception to this, however. If kids are questioning you when you count or asking, "Why, what did I do?", you need to refrain from responding (unless you really believe the student did not understand what he had done wrong). If you do slip and get into this kind of conversation, the resulting "dialogue" will inevitably lead to a power struggle—which is exactly what some students want. Remember the No Talking and No Emotion rules and you will get through these moments. There is no reason you cannot make an appointment to discuss the student's behavior at another time, if necessary (see chapter 19). Just don't converse when they are misbehaving.

CHAPTER SUMMARY

Elementary students seem to like 1-2-3 Magic. The program is predictable, easy to understand, and fair. All in all, students basically want to behave, even if they don't act like that sometimes. Few kids like being in trouble. This technique puts the responsibility for the student's behavior right where you want it—on the student rather than on the teacher.

25

MIDDLE SCHOOL

Using 1-2-3 Magic with Grades 6–8

CAN A METHOD AS simple as 1-2-3 Magic be used with a complicated, tricky, and often difficult group of adolescents? It sure can, and as a teacher, it may be just what you are looking for. Just because students stand a few feet taller, speak a few octaves lower, and appear a lot tougher, doesn't mean that the same basic human principles don't apply. Students in this stage of their lives continue to crave structure, consistency, and leadership. They also want you to be interested in them, and they continue to want a classroom environment where they can feel safe and thrive emotionally and academically.

Don't be fooled: the tough persona usually falls away once the noise and energy of the hallway subsides, classroom doors close, and the bell rings.

Laying the Foundation

Relationships

Before we discuss behavioral expectations, we must discuss relationships. This concept brings us back to our audience, our population: the wonderful teenagers in our lives. It is impossible to set up expectations and ask students to respect you and your classroom if you in turn do not respect them. Students at this age, especially, are keenly aware of your interest in them—or lack thereof. Why would you expect a teenager to show interest in you if you do not show interest in him? Your teaching all begins with the investment you are willing to make in your pupils as unique individuals. Adolescents sense who is on their side and who is an advocate for them, as opposed to who is out to give them a hard time. For example, on the first day of school (and each morning thereafter), greet students at the door, wear a big smile, and show an interest in each and every one. This may sound unrealistic and hard to do, but if it is a priority to you, it will happen. And it will be a worthwhile investment of your time.

> **Quick Tip**
>
> Teens are keenly aware of your interest—or lack of interest—in them. They sense who is on their side and who is not. On the first day of school, therefore, greet your students at the door. Smile and show an interest in each student.

Expect the kids to give you that teenage "What's her problem?" look, but keep it up! As your first class begins, spend some time getting to know your students before launching into the curriculum and your expectations for the year. Find out which school the kids attended last year, how many members there are in their families, and what their worst fears might be for the school year. By establishing these relationship-building anchors, a tone is automatically set in the room. Students feel they are important.

Then it is your turn to share yourself with your class. What are your fears, family information, and teaching history? This will make you "human" to students and set you apart from other teachers they may have encountered that first day. When students complete that first day of school, they will reflect on your class with a feeling of connection they may not have otherwise experienced. This will help build a solid, strong, and stable foundation for students to stand on both emotionally and academically. Those daunting first days of school—when you and the students are measuring each other up for the first time—are the perfect opportunity to lay the groundwork for how your classroom will look, feel, sound, and operate on a daily basis. This is the time when the "house expectations" are established. Gone are the days when rules such as "hands and feet to self" and "respect others" prevail. These are teenagers who have heard these rules throughout elementary school.

You should clarify expectations first and then develop a list of rules. Rules are secondary once the expectations are in place. Another key point is that if you share your class with an assistant or a team teacher, the expectations may not be yours alone. This is very important as you begin a year with two adults in the classroom. You should discuss your expectations together ahead of time before presenting them to students. If you can share in the presentation, it will be much more powerful because the students will know that all adults working in the classroom hold to these ideas. This is critical with teenagers because often these students are used to manipulating and "playing" parents against each other. You will get a lot of this same type of behavior in the classroom unless you and the other adult present a united front to the kids.

Expectations for Behavior

The first day any class meets, teachers usually go over the curriculum by reviewing a syllabus. This document will state the course objectives, any state benchmarks or targets of learning that will be covered, and the materials needed for the class. This moment is a perfect opportunity to include a brief written summary of your behavior policy. The points included in this policy will serve as your "discussion points" for the first few class meetings with the students.

Quick Tip

Power struggles regarding the use of electronic devices in schools have become a big issue these days. Make sure you have clear policies that you can use to back up your classroom discipline.

Although the behavior plan is written in a formal "policy" format, the group discussion and role-playing that should take place are crucial. Again, the longer you invest in setting up the rules, the less time you will spend enforcing them. Here is an example of a Kickoff Conversation with middle school students:

"I am so excited to be lucky enough to teach you. I have hope for you that you may not even have in yourself. Other teachers always laugh at me because I always brag I have the best kids, but honestly I usually do. You will get to know me very well throughout the year, as I will get to know you. It is important that I go over some 'house rules' with you so you have a better understanding of my expectations.

"I call this classroom my 'house' because most days I spend more time here than I do in my own home. When you look around, this isn't just a place I work—you see my belongings all around. I brought these items to school for us to share because I know you will enjoy them.

"Because this is my house, I have some expectations for you. I expect that you will always treat others, including me, with courtesy and respect. I expect that this classroom will remain neat and clean and that you will be a thoughtful citizen when you are in here. I expect you to raise your hand and wait patiently to be called on. I have no problem if you need to get up to get a tissue while I am speaking, but I do expect you to sharpen your pencils before class begins. If you are late to class, don't give me an excuse; you will be marked as unexcused tardy. *(Include any other expectations you may have.)*

"As far as behavior goes, here is how this house will operate. If you are disruptive in any way, you will receive a verbal 1. If you continue to be disruptive, you will receive a verbal 2. If you are having a bad day, and two warnings aren't enough for you to cease the disruptive behavior, you will receive a verbal 3 and be told to 'take five.'

"When this occurs, you are to proceed directly outside the

classroom door and sit on the floor until I let you know five minutes have passed. At that time, it is up to you to return on your
own back to class and continue with what other students are doing.
You will not be lectured; you will begin your work as if nothing
has happened.

"The benefit for you is that you will never hear me raise my
voice. I am not a screamer and refuse to let your bad day interrupt
my good day. If, however, 1-2-3 is needed again for you during
the same class period, it will happen a little differently. Instead
of going outside the classroom door at the count of 3, you will
be directed to the office to wait for the principal. This has never
happened in all of my years of teaching, so I highly doubt it will
happen this year, but just in case, you need to know my expectation of you. If you use inappropriate language in my class or
commit a worse offense, such as threatening or hitting a student,
you will go straight to 3 and go to the hallway to complete your
time-out. It is my discretion if I feel the offense warrants an immediate office visit. Any questions?"

At this point the teacher would role-play with another adult or
a student a few different scenarios. This is usually fun and breaks
the silence because teenagers love to role-play the "bad" behavior,
even if down deep they know that they may display the behavior at
some point. Enjoy this time, critique their acting, and don't forget
to laugh!

Group Incentives for Following Rules

This process may all be well and good if you have students who
mostly comply with teacher expectations. Each year, however, teachers experience students who take a little longer to catch up with their
peers when it comes to behavioral compliance. Assuming positive
reinforcement, ignoring, and intrinsic and extrinsic rewards have been
tried, it may be time to look for a group reward or incentive. This is

especially powerful with this age group because peers and peer pressure are a huge part of these kids' existence.

For example, if one student repeatedly needs to rely on 1-2-3 Magic, try to pair it with an incentive for the whole class. Here's how it might go:

> "I was thinking that it would be fun to do an activity each class period for the last ten minutes. Here is how this activity can be earned. Since we have a ninety-minute class period, I am going to break it down into three parts. If you receive a star for each thirty-minute segment, you will earn the ten-minute activity. Does anyone have any ideas of activities that might be fun?" *(Students then share different group games that you write on the overhead or the chalkboard.)*
>
> "So, can you all tell me again how this reward might be earned? Well, what happens if one student is really disruptive? Do we earn the star? It is important that you don't expect the star, because we all have bad days, right? If I hear anyone getting angry with the student who may have caused the class to not earn the star, the entire class will lose the privilege of trying to earn the ten-minute activity. Any questions?"

Usually, the silent peer pressure that exists in the room is enough for the one student who may be more behaviorally challenged to shape up. One may think that at this stage of development, students should not need this type of reward. Teachers have too much curriculum to get through to mess with silly incentives, right? Just remember that if you are having difficulty with behaviors, either individually or with whole classes, this will save you precious instructional time in the end. If class disruptions, outbursts, and general rudeness interrupt the flow of learning, five or ten minutes at the end of a period for classroom fun is not too much time to spend.

Remember that games can be highly educational, whether it be Charades, which uses expressive and receptive language skills; Jeopardy, which helps practice trivia regarding content-specific objectives; Hangman, which uses parts of the alphabet; or 7 Up, which works on social skills and interactions. These are all activities that gain educational time in a fun way. Reframe these pursuits as time gained, not time lost.

Counting the Whole Bunch

1-2-3 Magic is so adaptable that it can be used with individuals, small groups, and large groups. The 1-2-3 program can travel with a specific student in different educational settings, or it can hold up the walls to any size classroom. In a large class setting (thirty or more), counting can be used with students as individuals or as a whole class. Using the 1-2-3 program with a whole class will most likely occur during transition times. For example:

> "OK, class, we are now going to get our writing folders out and continue with the essay we began last class. If you could get your folders out of your binders, we will begin. *(As students do this, there is bound to be some small chatter.)* That's 1."

The class will quiet down, realizing the teacher expects this transitioning to be done quickly and quietly. Rarely in this situation should you need to proceed to a count of 2. If you must count to 2, and 3 follows, you could put in place any number of consequences. One that is particularly effective for this age group is time past the bell. If students waste your time getting materials out quietly or getting started at the beginning of class, then some of their social time in the hallway between classes will be lost. After all, this is where teenagers will feel it the most—time away from friends. This consequence happening once is usually enough for the number 1 to be taken very seriously.

If you find one student is consistently causing the class to be dismissed late, you may want to address this problem individually with that student during a lunchtime or after-school detention.

Working with these rapidly changing human beings that we call adolescents can be extremely rewarding. Watching a student blossom into the adult she will become is a life-changing event. But for a teacher, struggling and engaging in discipline conflicts day in and day out can be a negative career-changing event. Put some structure, consistency, and leadership in place using 1-2-3 Magic.

Keeping Track

When a student has five to seven different teachers and the consequences involve something that has taken place at a different time and outside the classroom, record keeping becomes a necessary evil. Teachers must also coordinate with the main office regarding exactly what a student has done and what consequence he is subject to.

Any record keeping must be as simple and clear as possible because it will be time-consuming. Computers and database software programs available today can help greatly with this process, but it still requires considerable staff time.

Two ideas can be helpful here: a Behavioral Accounting Form (or discipline slip) and a Behavioral Accounting (or Step) System. The Behavioral Accounting Form can be used by the classroom teacher for two purposes: to keep track of which student is at which point and to inform the office of what has happened. It needs to be brief so that filling it out does not disrupt class time unnecessarily.

Here's one possibility. The teacher fills in what the student did that generated each warning, such as talking, being out of her seat, bothering someone else, and so on. This is done right in class and right after the action occurred, but it is done in a calm, unobtrusive, and unchallenging manner. The "Third Occurrence" is no longer a warning, since it nets the consequence. If the student is to report to the office, she takes the slip with her to give to the assistant principal.

The form might look something like this:

Behavioral Accounting Form

Date:_____ _____

Student's Name:_ _____

FIRST WARNING:_____ _____

_____

SECOND WARNING:_____

_____

THIRD OCCURRENCE:_____

_____

Teacher Signature:_____ _____

The Behavioral Accounting System is kept by the main office and provides an orderly way for keeping track of the disciplinary history of each student. Incidents that occur represent "steps" on a progressive discipline and intervention program. It is important to keep in mind here that the purpose of such a system is evaluative and corrective, not primarily punitive. Any student who is continually running into trouble needs to be disciplined, but her life may also need to be examined more closely to try to determine what is going wrong.

The Behavioral Accounting (or Step) System provides for both discipline and evaluation. Each time an incident occurs, the student "progresses" to another defined point on the system, which serves the purpose of being a consequence (inevitably unpleasant). Each point, however, also defines an evaluation and planning function. Information is gathered about what might be happening to cause the trouble, and an attempt is made to make plans to eliminate the problems. A student can progress slowly (one step at a time) by accumulating "minor" infractions (e.g., tardies, referrals from class) or quickly (to the next "major" step) by engaging in more serious activities (e.g., fighting, smoking in school). A student can also receive an automatic 3 in class (skipping 1 and 2) and a "major" referral by doing something that the teacher considers to be very serious.

Here's what the Behavioral Accounting System might look like:

STEP SYSTEM

Minor Steps

1. Minor consequence
2.   " "
3.   " "
4.   " "

5. Major Step
   - Meeting with student, parents, and assistant principal
   - Plan for addressing problem

Minor Steps

6. Minor consequence
7.   " "

8. Major Step
   - Meeting with student, parents, and assistant principal or principal
   - Meeting of teacher team
   - Involvement of Special Services Team
   - Plan for addressing problem

Minor Steps

9. Minor consequence
10.   " "

11. Major Step
    - Case study or other thorough evaluation

The above system is a general plan for discipline, which can be modified by each school, according to its needs. It is also a good idea for the plan to be explained in the beginning of the school year and published in some kind of student handbook. The idea of "progressing" on the step system is itself something of a deterrent to students.

Students can go back "down" on the step system by going ten school days without any incident occurring. A student at step 9, for example, can go back to step 8. The interventions listed above, of course, do not kick in as the student goes back down. Most kids like the idea of this kind of positive reinforcement, and it also reduces their vulnerability to more "intrusive" interventions. Although it is beyond the scope of this book, a step system like this has also been used successfully at the high school level.

CHAPTER SUMMARY

1. Preteens and teens still appreciate structure, consistency, and leadership.
2. Try to show a genuine interest in each student.
3. Clarify your behavioral expectations on the first day.

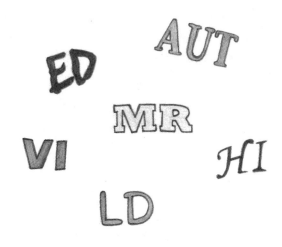

26

A NOTE ABOUT STUDENTS WITH SPECIAL NEEDS

Using 1-2-3 Magic for Students with Disabilities

ACCORDING TO THE INDIVIDUALS with Disabilities Education Improvement Act (IDEIA) of 2004, students with disabilities must have access to the general education curriculum. Today, many students with disabilities are included in general education classes at their neighborhood schools. All teachers, therefore, need to have the skills to work with all students. However, many teachers feel unprepared to work with all of the diverse learners in their classrooms, especially when it comes to behavior management.

1-2-3 Magic works well in general education classes as well as in specialized settings. As we mentioned in chapter 1, in order to benefit from 1-2-3 Magic, a child must have a cognitive age of at least two years. We have spoken with teachers who have used 1-2-3 Magic successfully with students with learning disabilities, emotional disabilities, autism, mild intellectual disabilities, and visual and/or hearing impairments. This chapter is meant to be a brief overview. There are entire books written on the subject of disabilities, and our intent here is to provide some basic information as it relates to the implementation of 1-2-3 Magic with some special populations in a school setting.

When working with students with disabilities (and all students, for that matter), it is important to work from their areas of strength. First, determine what the child can do or what he does respond to, and then build on those strengths. You may be working with a student, for instance, who is usually oppositional whenever you ask her to line up. She is usually cooperative, however, when it comes to helping other students. Is it possible to link the two activities? Perhaps your kids line up according to their table groups, and you make it clear to this student at these times that when she lines up appropriately, she is helping her group. Another approach with this girl might be to identify her as your helper. Give her the job of calling the tables to line up, so she is using her "power" in an appropriate way. As the teacher, you have the responsibility of helping students turn their negative behaviors into positive ones. One way to do this is to provide choices rather than engage in power struggles.

Each disability we'll discuss in this chapter has its own definition as well as certain, unique issues to keep in mind when applying 1-2-3 Magic.

Learning Disabilities

A learning disability (LD) is characterized by difficulties with language, reading, mathematics, attention, memory, thinking, reasoning, organization, and/or the generalization of skills. Many students with LD have social skills and behavioral skills commensurate with their general-education peers. Sometimes the processing deficits related to LD affect a student's social-emotional functioning and/or behavior in the classroom. Some students with LD need extra time to digest information. Therefore, it is important to provide "wait time" while they take in the message that you are sending. Teachers need to come up with ways to cue the students so they will pay attention to important information. Phrases such as "I am about to give a direction…" or "One, two, three, eyes on me…" prompt the students that they need to focus on the teacher. This approach helps to foster the habit of concentrating on key words, which helps students socially and academically. At first, the teacher must explicitly point out the key words ("Ready…," "Now…," "Next…") and perhaps reward students for responding appropriately by looking at the teacher.

It is also helpful to have students with LD repeat information you have just told them so you are sure they got the message. This is especially important in the "One Explanation" phase of the 1-2-3 program. Let's say David, a student with LD, is running in your classroom and you say, "David, you must walk in the classroom. Do you understand?" Hearing only the last part of your question and wanting to please you, David says, "Yes." Two seconds later, he is running again and you say, "That's 1." David responds, "What did I do? I wasn't doing anything."

> **Quick Tip**
> With an LD child, it's important to make sure he initially gets the message. Put yourself in close proximity, make eye contact, briefly explain the rule, and then have the youngster repeat the idea back to you.

To the casual observer, it looks like David is being argumentative and difficult. You told him the rule, he even said he understood it, and then he blatantly broke the rule right in front of you. But David did not process your explanation of the rule; it did not register with him. He was genuinely surprised to be counted. In the future, when an explanation to David is necessary, put yourself in close proximity to him, make eye contact, explain the rule in as few words possible, and have him repeat the concept to you. Another alternative would be to refer to a rules poster or some other visual reminder. In general, teachers have found that students with learning disabilities respond well to 1-2-3 Magic because it is very clear and also because they get a chance to correct their own behavior.

Emotional Disabilities

An emotional disability (ED) is characterized by problems with social behavior, inappropriate social skills, and/or lack of ownership of behavior.[2] Many students with emotional disabilities also have academic difficulties. Students with ED are masters at creating "the big splash" that we discussed in chapter 4. If an adult becomes overly emotional, it is often entertaining for these children, and the adult's outburst also takes the focus off them. When this happens, the student has a kind of negative control of the situation.

When working with students with ED, therefore, it is critically important to follow the No Talking and No Emotion rules. It is essential to attend to positive behavior and take little notice of negative behavior because a student with ED will often take attention any way she can get it. This does not mean that there will not be the usual consequences for bad behavior; it just means that the teacher will not get all worked up about it.

We know teachers who have practiced the 1-2-3 program in front of a mirror to make sure they have a blasé look when counting. Some teachers have even learned how to do a fake yawn they can use when a student is acting out. The trick is that the teacher must be aware of everything that is going on and also have a plan of action, while at the same time appearing as if she is almost indifferent to his behavior. This type of performance is certainly difficult when a student is calling you every name in the book, but it can be done!

For students with ED, the relationship between teacher and student is key. Students need to know they are safe and that they can trust you. Believe it or not, children want predictable, consistent limits even when they don't act like it. Sometimes these kids will test you by acting out to see what you will do. If you are caring, yet detached (a tricky combination!) and consistent, you will see your students responding to 1-2-3 Magic.

---

2.   For detailed information on managing children with ADHD, see Thomas W. Phelan, PhD, *All About ADHD*.

Quick Tip

Many students with emotional disabilities like to get teachers upset. But you want to have a plan of action while at the same time appearing almost indifferent to the student's misbehavior. Some teachers practice this in front of a mirror!

Many teachers are intimidated by students with ED. These students, however, are frequently acting out based on their own fears of inadequacy. Over time, in a warm yet demanding environment, the children learn that there are better ways to get attention and assistance. In order for this change in attitude to happen, 1-2-3 Magic is one piece of the larger picture. Other techniques must be incorporated into the classroom program to explicitly teach and reward the positive behavior. These other techniques might include daily, weekly, or monthly rewards for achieving goals as well as teaching self-monitoring procedures.

Mild Intellectual Disabilities

Intellectual disabilities (ID) involve deficits in intellectual functioning and delays in the areas of memory, attention, thinking, problem solving, and/or metacognition. There may also be issues with social behavior, language, and academic skills. Students with mild intellectual disabilities (MID) can benefit from 1-2-3 Magic, though they will need clear and simple directions and lots of repetition.

If a student with MID is acting out, the teacher sometimes needs to take the time to understand what triggered the behavior. She should ask herself, "Was the task too difficult for this student?", "What is the student trying to communicate?", or "Does he have the language and communication skills to express emotions, wants, needs, or frustrations?"

As the teacher addresses the behavior, she needs to keep all concepts concrete. Prior to starting 1-2-3 Magic, the teacher should target one or two specific Stop behaviors. Because students with MID benefit a lot from visuals, the teacher might create a simple book showing 1-2-3 Magic in action for that student. The pages of this book addressing appropriate language, for example, might have simple pictures and text such as:

Page 1: Sam uses nice words.

Page 2: If Sam says bad words, his teacher says, "3."

Page 3: On 3, Sam goes to time-out.

Page 4: Sam sits quietly in time-out and waits for the bell to ring.

Page 5: When the bell rings, Sam comes back to the group.

Page 6: Sam uses nice words.

A "story" such as this helps the student to understand the procedure. It also allows the child to become responsible for his behavior by making smart choices. Another key component in these situations is teaching alternate behaviors. In the story above, for instance, it is emphasized that Sam should use "nice words." These words need to be identified for him, and when he uses them, he should be positively reinforced.

Autism

Autism is typically characterized by deficits in communication and social functioning. Autism is a spectrum disorder, and there is a wide range of abilities within this continuum. Students with autism who are included in general education classes, for example, may have been diagnosed with Asperger's Disorder, a form of higher functioning autism.

Students with autism frequently have difficultly connecting and communicating with others. These kids may have trouble with expressive and receptive language, which can be very frustrating for them. For these reasons, it is essential to use visuals when working with students with autism. For some students, it is enough to pair the 1-2-3 count with the same number of fingers. For others students, however, pictures or a chart must be used. Other concrete examples of counters include numbered blocks, numbered cards, and cards with smiling and frowning faces.

There are several steps you can take ahead of time to help students with autism become aware of your classroom rules and consequences.

These steps often serve as preventive measures as well. One important step, for example, is to set up an organized environment and post a visual schedule. Pictures of students following the rules can be referenced frequently. The teacher may wish to make a set of pictures or symbols to carry throughout the day to remind the student what to do. If a student is about to leave the room without permission, for instance, the teacher could say the student's name and hold up a picture representing staying in the room to remind the student of the rule.

Simple pictures might also be used to help a student communicate. If you are giving a student a choice of juice or milk, for example, you could have a picture of each and have him point to what he wants. For students who can read, words can be used instead of pictures. In some cases it is effective to put short directions in writing instead of telling the student what to do. Students with autism sometimes cannot read facial expressions, body language, or tone of voice. The written words, therefore, may be more effective than talking. Another option is using sign language after you have taught the student a few signs (sit, stop, good, and so on).

If a student with autism is acting out, she needs to know exactly what she is doing wrong. Sometimes she is not aware of what she is doing or that it is even a problem. This, of course, does not mean that you should give her a lecture, but you do need to find a clear, concise way to tell or show her that she is breaking a rule. Consistency is critical here. You need to use the same word or symbol every time for rules, counting, and consequences.

In many cases, students with autism will resist the initial implementation of 1-2-3 Magic because it is something new and different. You may see behavior getting worse before it gets better, but consistency will be your ally. Over time, if you stick with the consequences, the students will learn to make connections between their actions and the results. For children with autism, however, it is also important to individualize your techniques to some extent. One teacher, for example, told us about a student who screamed and yelled when told to go to time-out, but who had no problem going to the "thinking area" for five minutes.

Visual and/or Hearing Impairments

A visual impairment may be present when an individual has limited visual acuity, which can range from mild to severe. Some students with visual impairments may need accommodations such as enlarged images and print, while others may need to use the Braille system. Students with visual impairments tend to rely on their senses of sound and touch to gain information about the world around them.

The identification of a hearing impairment is based on an assessment of hearing ability. Hearing impairments can also range from mild to severe, with some individuals classified as hard of hearing and others as deaf. Students with hearing impairments may have academic delays because of their difficulty processing language. Difficulties with communication may also impact relationships with others.

Again, the message is to build on the student's strengths and abilities. For a student with a visual impairment, it is obviously important to use the auditory and tactile channels for communicating information. You might pair a verbal message with something sensory, such as handing the student a card on each count. On the other hand, for a student with a hearing impairment, it would make sense to use visual cues such as fingers, pictures, a chart, and signs.

Students with special needs usually respond to 1-2-3 Magic in a positive way. When implemented well and with creativity, 1-2-3 Magic can help both the teacher and the student feel more comfortable because they each know what to expect. Remember, even if they do not always act like it, children benefit from firm and consistent limits. And setting limits also shows your students that you care.

CHAPTER SUMMARY

1-2-3 Magic, when implemented well and with creativity, can be just as effective for students with special needs as for neurotypical students.

||||| **PART VII** |||||

Collaborating with Administrators

CHAPTER 27
Administrative Policy and Teacher Support

CHAPTER 28
Teacher Self-Evaluation Checklist

27

ADMINISTRATIVE POLICY AND TEACHER SUPPORT

How Teachers and Administrators Can Work Together

ONE OF THE MORE difficult parts of a school administrator's job involves establishing and maintaining an effective discipline policy. This task includes supporting one's teachers, providing assistance to teachers whose skills need improvement, and at the same time being fair to students and parents. Not an easy assignment at all! In this chapter we ask a former school principal some direct and pointed questions.

How does an administrator support teachers in discipline?

It is the principal's job to make sure that the division's regulations/policies are being followed and that teachers are implementing school-wide behavior standards. In that context, principals must assist teachers by supporting their classroom management procedures. As the competence of the teachers may vary, the level of principal intervention may vary:

Excellent Teacher: The principal will confer with the teacher behind the scenes and concur with the teacher before students; the principal will be available to collaborate when asked; and the principal will use this teacher as a mentor for others needing help with behavior management.

Average Teacher: The principal will review with this teacher her rationale for her classroom management system; the principal may need to observe and give feedback and encouragement; and the principal will suggest training opportunities to increase management skills.

Ineffective Teacher: The principal will need to have direct intervention in the development/implementation of a classroom management plan; the principal may need to bring in a specialist or model teacher for mentoring; the principal will need to do frequent observations and give written feedback; and the evaluation system should address behavior management.

How does a principal manage an authoritarian vs. an overly permissive type of teacher?

Both types need to move toward a combination of nurturing and authority. The authoritarian type may find it very difficult to avoid the struggle for control and would need a discussion of the need for "warm switch on." The overly permissive type may have the opposite problem, not feeling comfortable implementing consequences for inappropriate behavior. Encouragement toward a "demanding switch on" would be appropriate. 1-2-3 Magic provides the principal with a nonthreatening explanation to offer the teacher.

What do administrators tell teachers about referrals to the office?

Principals must provide teachers with guidelines for office referrals. School divisions have discipline regulations that clarify certain issues that must be handled by an administrator. A mechanism should be established for this type of mandatory office referral.

These serious issues aside, principals must also be readily available to teachers for collaboration in using the office referral. The office referral should occur only when the teacher has exhausted her resources for behavior change. Excessive reliance on the principal's authority serves to diminish the teacher's authority. Principals should give teachers behind-the-scenes feedback regarding overuse of office referrals.

What should a principal do with a student when he is referred? Can an office referral backfire and be reinforcement of bad behavior?

School divisions generally define consequences for serious discipline offenses, and principals are required to follow the regulations. However, many of the behavior issues facing teachers are not specifically addressed by these behavior regulations. These problems often result in office referrals, which must be handled collaboratively by the teacher and principal. This collaboration may include the decision that the student is avoiding the classroom and, thus, the office referral is not appropriate. As a result of repeated office referrals, a student may become comfortable there and prefer the office to the classroom. Teachers and principals need to address the purpose of the referral, the consequences imposed by the principal, and the desired behavior change.

When should the administration get involved with parents?

Principals have direct contact with parents about serious violations of the discipline regulations. Otherwise, they should be available for contact whenever asked by either the teacher or the parent. Teachers need to build working relationships with the parents so that principal intervention is not regularly needed.

How do you evaluate a teacher's classroom discipline, given that you never get to see it much and the kids probably behave better when the principal is in the room?

Students in a classroom with a poor disciplinarian in charge are rarely able to behave all of a sudden when the principal is around! These classrooms have higher rates of office referrals, discipline code violations, parent complaints about misbehaviors, and lower work production. The necessary information is there if you know where to look and take the time to look for it.

How do you define rules and general school policies for teachers and students? How much leeway do teachers have in interpreting this?

The school division and the principal define the school behavior regulations, and these regulations should be distributed to both parents and students at the beginning of each school year. The teacher is responsible for making sure that all students have the opportunity to understand the regulations through classroom activities. Additionally, teachers have the responsibility for establishing rules for classroom operations.

An angry parent calls saying that her child has a "screamer" for a teacher and this is aggravating the child's anxiety disorder. You agree the teacher does yell a lot. What do you do?

Direct intervention by the principal is called for in this instance. Conferencing with the teacher regarding the complaint is a good place to start. In this meeting, you impart information about anxiety disorders, discuss a self-monitoring plan for the teacher, and then follow up with drop-in observations to monitor the teacher's progress in reducing yelling.

A shy, passive parent calls saying that her child has a "screamer" for a teacher and this is aggravating the child's anxiety disorder. You don't agree with the parent that the teacher is overly harsh. What do you do?

Assure the parent that you will investigate, explaining that you have not experienced this teacher as a screamer. Do drop-in visits and contact parent to report that no screaming was observed. If the parent continues to complain, arrange a conference with the teacher and parents and a clinical staff member, and initiate a discussion of how a student with severe anxiety disorder may experience a classroom and how a teacher could help with the problem. It is essential that the parent be heard and the teacher not be faulted. It is also essential that you keep an open mind and allow the data you collect and the observations you make to alter your original opinions if necessary.

What are the biggest gripes administrators have about teachers regarding discipline?

The gripes heard most often from administrators about teachers are these: the classroom discipline is not consistent; the discipline is too often reactive rather than proactive; and the behavior expectations are unrealistic—either too high or too low.

What are the biggest gripes teachers have about administrators regarding discipline?

The gripes heard most often from teachers about administrators are lack of follow-through and acquiescence to parents' demands.

You get a lot of complaints from teachers and parents that Mr. or Mrs. So-and-So has lost control of the classroom. What do you do?

Assure the complainers that you will investigate. Make drop-in visits, check referral rates, and have a discussion with the teacher in order to gain vital information as to the nature of problems in the classroom. If you conclude that the complaints have merit, it's time to begin working directly with the teacher on a plan for improvement.

What should be done differently regarding students with special needs when it comes to discipline?

It is always necessary to examine how a student's disability impacts his or her behavior. This does not mean lowering behavior expectations! It simply means adapting the learning experience so that these students can meet the behavior expectations.

How does 1-2-3 Magic help?

1-2-3 Magic provides school staff and parents with an effective way to manage the behavior of children in order to discourage negative behavior and encourage positive behavior. The principles of 1-2-3 Magic (No Talking, No Emotion, the Little Adult Assumption, Positive Reinforcement, and so on) foster feelings of calm and self-assurance in the teacher, which has a positive effect on her relationship with her students and their parents as well as other staff members. Teachers who use 1-2-3 Magic feel proud of what is going on in their classrooms and feel energized by their ability to handle problems as they arise.

What are the keys to hiring the "right" teachers in the first place?

School administrators know well that an effective behavior management program must begin with committed and competent teachers! Selecting the right teacher is the key to success of 1-2-3 Magic in a school, so we will review some of the most important "teacher qualities" to look for in hiring school staff and how these qualities might be determined in the interview process.

Effective teachers will demonstrate a high level of self-confidence. Look for teachers who are comfortable in the following roles: instructional leader, role model, and parent liaison. These are people who talk enthusiastically about their successes and failures, with no hesitation in acknowledging their mistakes. They demonstrate a willingness to listen and learn from others and are continuously looking for "another way" to help students. These folks are never afraid to say, "I don't know, but I'll try to find out!"

During an initial job interview, these are the people who usually:

- Give you significant eye contact and have relaxed body language
- Are comfortable with your leading the conversation; do not attempt to impress with prepared materials
- React well to open-ended questions regarding their training and work experience
- Listen to what you are saying and respond appropriately
- Relate experiences in which they have had to look beyond the existing circumstances and create alternatives for change

Here are some suggested interview questions:

1. Describe one of the most difficult behavior problems you have handled and how it was resolved.
2. Tell me about your previous teaching experience.
3. You have had a very difficult day with Joe's disruptive behavior and have attempted to relate this to Joe's mother by phone. She desperately says, "I can't do anything with him." How would you respond?

A high level of self-awareness is essential to being a successful teacher. When setting limits for students and implementing consistent and appropriate consequences, one's own emotions are greatly impacted. Directly stated: If I can't manage my own anger, how can I be a model for students? It is critical that a successful behavior manager be aware of her own anger thresholds and triggers. Effective behavior management is always proactive—not reactive—and the decisions we make for students must be driven by concern for their growth and not by our own anger and frustration.

Suggested interview questions in this regard:

1. How would you feel if, at the end of a very difficult day in the classroom, the administrator requested that you respond to a critical inquiry from the parents of one of your students? What would be your response?
2. How do you know when you have reached the outer limits of your patience with a difficult student who continues to defy your authority? Can you feel yourself getting angry? What do you do?

A person who expresses a real commitment to teaching will inevitably be the person who invests the most in the job role. These people express the desire to be the best possible professional educator and are willing to involve themselves in learning activities to continuously increase their teaching skills. This may involve continued formal education and/or observation and consultation with other teachers. It is important to make sure that a teacher candidate has appropriate educational credentials and has had training opportunities for gaining skills in behavior management. This training and education should have provided knowledge of content curriculum, human development, and interpersonal skills. (Be sure to check applicant's recommendations.)

At the job interview, dedicated teachers will usually:

- Demonstrate good conversational skills
- Exhibit goods social skills; e.g., punctual to interview, appropriately dressed, respectful to interviewer
- Appropriately advise you of their accomplishments

As any educator knows, students watch what we do, not what we say! Good teachers must demonstrate respect and compassion for others. Modeling of respectful behavior is critical to the success of any management program. Although teachers need to maintain boundaries between themselves and their students, compassion must always be a guiding force when implementing limits and consequences.

What should administrators look for regarding classroom structure and engagement of students?

Effective educators are prepared, actively involved, clear, and consistent. Administrators need to set the expectation that teachers plan lessons that will engage all students. It is important for teachers to structure the lessons so that all students can learn the material. Differentiated instruction that taps into the different learning styles of students should be encouraged. Administrators should also look for each teacher to have her classroom set up in a way that minimizes distraction and allows for the teacher to circulate among the students to "troubleshoot" academically or behaviorally. Another item that should be clear and posted is a list of rules and procedures for the classroom. It can be helpful to have a picture cue next to the written description. Students are more likely to follow the rules and procedures if the kids participate in role-plays when they are introduced, they are clear, and they are reviewed regularly.

How will an observer know if a teacher is addressing Stop behaviors correctly?

If there are few acting-out behaviors, and the few that do occur are stopped by a count of 1 or 2, the teacher is probably doing the 1-2-3 procedure correctly. Administrators should see a teacher who is calm yet clear when counting her students. It is critical to remember the No Talking and the No Emotion rules. The only words you should hear when the teacher is counting are "That's 1," "That's 2," and occasionally "That's 3, take five." The counting should occur when a student is engaged in an undesirable behavior such as whining, talking out, arguing, and so on. Of course, the key to any system of discipline is consistency. In order for the teacher to stay on top of the behavior of many students, she needs to have a system for keeping track of counts. Some teachers do this in their heads, some have colored cards, and others use a stoplight. Whatever the system is, it is important for the administrator to see a teacher who is not confused and keeps track of the behavior of her students.

What will an observer see if a teacher is using Start behavior techniques?

In the case of Start behavior, what we want to see is a teacher who is not quiet when her students are. In other words, when students are doing what they are supposed to do, the teacher should offer praise to specific students and/or the whole class. She should do this frequently—much more often than she redirects students regarding misbehavior. The teacher should tailor her praise to the age group and personality of her students. She can give praise in ways to ensure that other students may hear it and benefit. She can also praise students to other adults in front of the ones receiving the compliment. You will see this teacher going out of her way to find positive words for all of her students.

How will an administrator know that the teacher is working to build a positive relationship with her students?

An administrator knows that the teacher is working on positive relationships with her students if he sees the teacher praising the students often and enjoying her time with them. This teacher creates a classroom in which it is fun to learn. She is a forgiving person, although she takes inappropriate behavior seriously and does not approve of it; she doles out the consequences and moves on so that the student has an opportunity to do the same. She is an empathetic listener and makes time to talk with her students one on one whenever possible. Because of these efforts, she knows which students are on the soccer team, who has a new baby brother, who wants to be a doctor, and who cheers for the local sports team.

What should an administrator expect from a teacher with regard to contacting parents?

Since the home/school connection is so important, it is helpful to have a teacher who makes the effort to call parents whether they have a positive or negative situation to discuss. This teacher is able to separate a child from his negative behavior, and she can sum up what is happening at school in a clear and concise manner. She also uses sympathetic listening to hear about what is going on at home. The collaboration between this teacher and the parents of her students is strengthened by the fact that she shared 1-2-3 Magic with them early in the year and has answered questions about how to implement the program successfully at home.

28

TEACHER SELF-EVALUATION CHECKLIST

Recognizing Your Strengths and Weaknesses in the Classroom

FROM TIME TO TIME it's helpful to take a long, hard look at yourself and your teaching style. This chapter will help you do that in an organized way using the principles we've discussed already in *1-2-3 Magic in the Classroom*.

So take a deep breath and rate your actual daily work and behavior as a teacher on the following items using this scale:

5—**Excellent**
4—**Good**
3—**Average**
2—**Below Average**
1—**Poor**

After you have completed your ratings, we'll show you how to transform some of the numbers you've produced into a kind of description of yourself in terms of the four different teaching styles we described earlier: authoritarian, detached, permissive, and authoritative. Keep in mind that though no rating system is perfect, it can be helpful in suggesting areas for growth and continuing education.

A. Structure, engagement, and monitoring of students and their work (preventive discipline)

Let's begin with the education/academic part of the teaching job itself. We mentioned earlier that a student who is doing his work will not be a behavior problem. How well do you do in terms of structuring your pupils' work, engaging them in the learning process, and monitoring their performance? Below, circle the number that you feel best describes your performance for each item:

5 4 3 2 1   **Prepared lesson plans**

5 4 3 2 1   **Teacher activity and circulation**

5 4 3 2 1   **Effective seating plan**

5 4 3 2 1   **Rules and procedures explained/posted**

5 4 3 2 1   **Rules and procedures role-played**

5 4 3 2 1   **Actively engages students in work and learning**

5 4 3 2 1   **Monitors students' work and behavior**

5 4 3 2 1   **Makes adjustments based on monitoring**

Now add up all your ratings and enter that number here:

Divide that total by 8 and enter the result here:

This last number represents your average or overall rating for our preventive discipline dimension. How does it measure up on our basic rating scale?

5—Excellent
4—Good
3—Average
2—Below Average
1—Poor

B. Parent contact

Another important—and by no means easy—part of the teaching job has to do with parent contact. Getting along and communicating regularly with your kids' parents (or other caretakers) can help or hinder your effectiveness with classroom discipline. How well do you do when it comes to picking up the phone, emailing, or face-to-face contacts? Below, circle the number that you feel best describes your performance for each item:

5 4 3 2 1   Calls or emails parents with good news

5 4 3 2 1   Not afraid to contact parents with bad news

5 4 3 2 1   Clarifies problem behavior well

5 4 3 2 1   Encourages use of 1-2-3 at home when necessary

5 4 3 2 1   Orients parents to 1-2-3 in beginning of year

5 4 3 2 1   Listens sympathetically to parents

5 4 3 2 1   Brainstorms solutions with parents

5 4 3 2 1   Firm but nonjudgmental with moms and dads

Now add up all your ratings and enter that number here:

Divide that total by 8 and enter the result here:

This last number represents your average or overall rating for our parent contact dimension. How does it measure up on our basic rating scale?

5—Excellent
4—Good
3—Average
2—Below Average
1—Poor

Step 1: Managing undesirable behavior (Stop behavior)

Now let's look at our three discipline steps, beginning with the management of undesirable behavior, or Stop behavior. Keeping difficult, irritating, and disruptive behavior in line is critical to having a productive classroom. This kind of order is also essential if you are going to enjoy your youngsters. Below, circle the number that you feel best describes your performance for each item:

5 4 3 2 1   **Clear Counts**

5 4 3 2 1   **Consistency**

5 4 3 2 1   **System for keeping track of counts**

5 4 3 2 1   **No extra talking**

5 4 3 2 1   **No extra emotion**

5 4 3 2 1   **No excessive ignoring of negative behavior**

5 4 3 2 1   Behavior counted is clear

5 4 3 2 1   Can manage/calm entire class when necessary

Now add up all your ratings and enter that number here: ☐

Divide that total by 8 and enter the result here: ☐

This last number represents your average or overall rating for managing undesirable behavior. How does it measure up on our basic rating scale?

5—Excellent
4—Good
3—Average
2—Below Average
1—Poor

Step 2: Encouraging positive behavior (Start behavior)

Next we'll look at your ability to help motivate the kids to do the good things you want them to do, such as doing schoolwork, lining up, transitioning smoothly, paying attention, and cleaning up. You recall that Start behavior takes more motivation on the part of your students, and therefore it's also going to be more work for you! Below, circle the number that you feel best describes your performance for each item:

5 4 3 2 1   Frequent use of praise

5 4 3 2 1   Across-the-room praise

5 4 3 2 1   Next door praise

5 4 3 2 1   Cheerful, encouraging manner

5 4 3 2 1   Reinforcement not just for a few students

5 4 3 2 1   Good behavior is not ignored

5 4 3 2 1   Positive comments exceed corrective

5 4 3 2 1   Use of cross dialogue when helpful

Now add up all your ratings and enter that number here: ☐

Divide that total by 8 and enter the result here: ☐

This last number represents your average or overall rating for managing undesirable behavior. How does it measure up on our basic rating scale?

5—Excellent
4—Good
3—Average
2—Below Average
1—Poor

Step 3: Your relationship with your students

You want to get along well with your students while still being an effective boss. Though your classroom is not a democracy, you want to be warm and supportive, to be a good listener, and to have fun with your students. You also want to start each day with a clean slate, doing your best not to hold grudges for past misbehavior. Below, circle the number that you feel best describes your performance for each item:

5 4 3 2 1   Praise

5 4 3 2 1   Enjoys students

5 4 3 2 1   **Builds fun into school day, work, and activities**

5 4 3 2 1   **Forgiveness: doesn't carry grudges**

5 4 3 2 1   **Good listener when appropriate**

5 4 3 2 1   **Takes personal interest in students**

5 4 3 2 1   **Welcomes kids in the morning**

5 4 3 2 1   **Uses one-on-one conferences well**

Now add up all your ratings and enter that number here: ☐

Divide that total by 8 and enter the result here: ☐

This last number represents your average or overall rating for managing undesirable behavior. How does it measure up on our basic rating scale?

5—Excellent
4—Good
3—Average
2—Below Average
1—Poor

Interpreting Your Scores

Your scores on steps 1, 2, and 3 give us some hints as to how you might be characterizing your overall teaching style. High scores (4s and 5s) on step 1, for example, would indicate that you are good at the demanding side of the teaching equation. Low scores on step 1 mean that you need to work harder to keep your students' difficult behavior in line.

High scores on step 3, on the other hand, mean that you put a lot of effort into getting along with your students. You are warm, gentle, and supportive. Low scores on step 3 indicate that you need some improvement in your relationship with the youngsters in your classroom.

Step 2 is a kind of combination of both the warm and the demanding aspects of teaching. Praise is a good example of this combination. Praise is warm and friendly, but it also means *keep up the good work*—a subtle demand.

Here is a format for interpreting your scores for steps 1, 2, and 3 in terms of the teaching style categorizations we mentioned earlier in chapter 5. Here is what you might expect for each teaching style:

	Scores		
	Step 1	**Step 2**	**Step 3**
Permissive	1	3	5
Authoritarian	5	3	1
Detached	1	1	1
Authoritative	5	5	5

How did you describe yourself? What are your teaching strengths, and where might you need to do some work?

PART VIII

Looking Forward

CHAPTER 29
Enjoying Your New Classroom

29

ENJOYING YOUR
NEW CLASSROOM

How 1-2-3 Magic Will Change
Your Teaching Experience

AT THIS POINT YOU are well into our three steps. You are controlling undesirable behavior with counting; you are using the Start behavior tactics to encourage good behavior (and have come up with a few of your own); and you are consistently working on building your relationship with each of your students by means of praise, fun, forgiveness, and listening.

1-2-3 Magic is known for producing results. It works—and it often works in a very short period of time. No magic. Just the logical, consistent application of certain basic principles to the nth degree. Just one more caution, though, before we let you go.

Falling Off the Wagon

Nobody is perfect. Teachers are human beings who have good days and bad days. Many educators have used the 1-2-3 program religiously for years and years. For others, however, it is a struggle to stay consistent and to keep in mind what they're supposed to be doing.

The struggle we're talking about here is called "slipping." Some people call it backsliding. It means you start out well with 1-2-3 Magic and get the kids shaped up, but then you slip back into old unproductive ways of operating. The 1-2-3 switch sort of goes to the OFF position. The former status quo has a nasty way of sneaking back up on us. Falling off the wagon can occur suddenly on an especially bad day, or slipping can happen more gradually over a period of months or even years.

In the course of a day, there's always so much going on. You have papers to grade, meetings to attend, and parents to call. When you're trying to do nine things at once, who can remember the No Talking and No Emotion rules?

You can! It's not always easy, but it beats screaming and arguing, which only add to your troubles, making you feel angry and guilty on top of everything else. Remember: 1-2-3 Magic was specifically created for busy adults like yourself who are inevitably going to get upset and distracted from time to time.

Over the long term, slipping can occur for a number of reasons. The most frequent culprits are illness, changes in schedule, new students, and plain forgetfulness. Gradually, you may find yourself starting to talk more and more, and then you start getting too excited and frustrated. Suddenly, it seems, you are not enjoying your class anymore. Then one night, you wake up at 3:00 and wonder, "What happened to the 1-2-3 method?"

What do you do when you find yourself—over the short or long term—falling back into your old ways? First of all, accept slipping as normal. Nobody's perfect, including you, and you shouldn't expect yourself to be. And teaching young children is a complicated job.

Second, get back to 1-2-3 Magic basics. Almost invariably, when an adult comes to us and says, "The 1-2-3 program is not working anymore," what is happening is a major violation of the No Talking and No Emotion rules. This point cannot be emphasized strongly enough. Sit down and review the 1-2-3 Magic theory and the procedures very carefully, and then get back on track.

Fortunately, the Stop and Start behavior methods described here are simple and can be resurrected and reapplied with little difficulty. The fact that you've used them once and slipped up does not hurt their effectiveness the second time around. Turn that 1-2-3 switch back to ON.

When you have caught yourself backsliding on a bad day, you might say something like this to your class: "Guys, I'm not doing my job right. I am frustrated and I'm talking and arguing too much. We're going back to counting as of right now." When you've regressed over a longer period, consider redoing the Kickoff Conversation and then do some role-playing with the whole class.

Over the course of the year, you may go through a number of slips and recoveries—daily, weekly, or monthly. Each time you catch yourself getting careless, just pick yourself up, take a deep breath, and go back to what you know works best.

A Different Future

What can you expect from 1-2-3 Magic? You can expect a more peaceful classroom, less arguing, less misbehavior, and fewer angry moments. You can also expect that more learning will take place. There will be more time for work and fun, and praise will come more easily to you. The self-esteem of your students will improve. So will your self-esteem because you will be more in control and will know you are handling things correctly. As a teacher, you will feel more confident, more in control of your class, and you will have more time for instruction.

What it all boils down to is this: how do you want to spend your time? One option is that you can spend your time like this:

Before 1-2-3 Magic, the kids are driving you crazy most of the time. You are caught up in frequent but futile attempts at "discipline." There is little time to enjoy the children, educate them, or even like them.

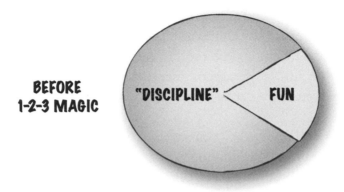

On the other hand, you can spend your time like this:

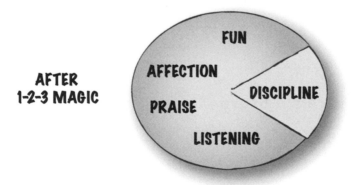

In this situation, the proper perspective has been established. Sanity is restored by the 1-2-3 program, making discipline crisp, gentle, and efficient. There's less arguing and yelling, and in this more peaceful atmosphere, there are more good times. Everyone's self-esteem benefits.

We remember one teacher a few years back who had truly given up. Her class was out of control and she did not know what to do. On one particular day, a student had actually thrown a calculator at her. This young woman had tried every discipline trick she could think of, but her students were consistently fighting, talking back, and doing little academic work. The teacher was ready to quit. At this low point, a compassionate colleague recommended 1-2-3 Magic, and our teacher tried it out of sheer desperation. Lo and behold, it worked—and in relatively short order! You, too, can make discipline less exhausting in your classroom. Good luck!

APPENDIX

Further Reading and Resources

Baker, Jed. *No More Meltdowns: Positive Strategies for Managing and Preventing Out-of-Control Behavior.* Future Horizons, 2008.

Greene, Ross W. *The Explosive Child: A New Approach for Understanding and Parenting Easily Frustrated, Chronically Inflexible Children,* 5th ed. Harper Paperbacks, 2014.

Greene, Ross W. *Lost at School: Why Our Kids with Behavioral Challenges Are Falling through the Cracks and How We Can Help Them,* 2nd ed. Scribner, 2014.

Lemov, Doug. *Teach Like a Champion: 49 Techniques that Put Students on the Path to College (K–12).* Jossey-Bass, 2010.

Long, Nicholas James, and Mary M. Wood. *Life Space Intervention: Talking with Children and Youth in Crisis.* Pro-Ed, 1990.

Mandel, Joey. *Moment to Moment: A Positive Approach to Managing Classroom Behavior.* Pembroke Publishers, 2013.

Smith, Rick. *Conscious Classroom Management: Unlocking the Secrets of Great Teaching.* Conscious Teaching Publications, 2004.

Wong, Harry K., and Rosemary T. Wong. *The First Days of School: How to Be an Effective Teacher.* Harry K. Wong Publications, 2004.

Resources for Parents

EMOTIONAL INTELLIGENCE

Borba, Michele. *Building Moral Intelligence: The Seven Essential Virtues That Teach Kids to Do the Right Thing.* San Francisco: Jossey-Bass, 2002.

Goleman, Daniel. *Emotional Intelligence: Why It Can Matter More Than IQ.* New York: Bantam Books, 2005.

ACTIVE LISTENING AND PROBLEM SOLVING

Faber, Adele, and Elaine Mazlish. *How to Talk So Kids Will Listen and Listen So Kids Will Talk.* New York: Scribner, 2012.

Ginott, Haim. *Between Parent and Child.* Revised and updated by Alice Ginott and H. Wallace Goddard. New York: Crown Publishing, 2003.

CHILDHOOD EMOTIONAL PROBLEMS

Chansky, Tamar E. *Freeing Your Child from Anxiety: Powerful, Practical Solutions to Overcome Your Child's Fears, Worries, and Phobias.* New York: Crown Publishing, 2014.

Coloroso, Barbara. *The Bully, the Bullied, and the Bystander: From Preschool to High School—How Parents and Teachers Can Help Break the Cycle.* New York: William Morrow Paperbacks, 2009.

Turecki, Stanley, and Sarah Warnick. *The Emotional Problems of Normal Children: How Parents Can Understand and Help.* New York: Bantam Books, 1994.

SEPARATION AND DIVORCE

Philyaw, Deesha, and Michael D. Thomas. *Co-Parenting 101: Helping Your Kids Thrive in Two Households after Divorce*. Oakland, CA: New Harbinger, 2013.

Ricci, Isolina. *The CoParenting Toolkit: The Essential Supplement for Mom's House, Dad's House*. La Vergne, TN: Lightning Source, 2015.

TECH AND MEDIA

Awareness Technologies. WebWatcherKids website, www.webwatcher kids.com (*Information on monitoring software*)

Common Sense Media website, www.commonsensemedia.org (*One-stop shop for reviews on TV, movies, music, games, books, and websites— excellent resource*)

McAfee. InternetSafety website, www.internetsafety.com (*Safe Eyes Internet filter*)

National Center for Missing and Exploited Children. NetSmartz website, www.netsmartz.org (*Very popular safety site used by educators, law enforcement, and parents*)

WiredSafety website, www.wiredsafety.org (*Internet safety site*)

PARENTING STYLES

Cohen, Lawrence J. *The Opposite of Worry: The Playful Parenting Approach to Childhood Anxieties and Fears*. New York: Ballantine Books, 2013.

Miles, Karen. *The Power of Loving Discipline*. New York: Penguin, 2006.

Semmelroth, Carl. *The Anger Habit in Parenting: A New Approach to Understanding and Resolving Family Conflict*. Naperville, IL: Sourcebooks, 2005.

Stiffelman, Susan. *Parenting with Presence: Practices for Raising Conscious, Confident, Caring Kids*. Novato, CA: New World Library, 2015.

CHILD TEMPERAMENT

Borsky, Bari. *Authentic Parenting: A Four Temperaments Guide to Understanding Your Child—And Yourself!* Herndon, VA: SteinerBooks, 2013.

Dodson, James C. *The New Strong-Willed Child.* Carol Stream, IL: Tyndale Momentum, 2014.

OTHER DISCIPLINE ALTERNATIVES

Farber, Adele, and Elaine Mazlish. *Siblings without Rivalry: How to Help Your Children Live Together So You Can Live Too.* New York: W. W. Norton & Company, 2012.

Leman, Kevin. *Have a New Kid by Friday! How to Change Your Child's Attitude, Behavior & Character in 5 Days.* Grand Rapids, MI: Revell, 2012.

MacKenzie, Robert J. *Setting Limits with Your Strong-Willed Child: Eliminating Conflict by Establishing Clear, Firm, and Respectful Boundaries.* New York: Three Rivers Press, 2013.

Markham, Laura. *Peaceful Parent, Happy Kids: How to Stop Yelling and Start Connecting.* New York: Perigee, 2012.

RESEARCH ON 1-2-3 MAGIC

Allen, Sharon M., Roy H. Thompson, and Jane Drapeaux. "Successful Methods for Increasing and Improving Parent and Child Interactions." Paper presented at the 24th Annual Training Conference of the National Head Start Association, Boston, May 25–31, 1997.

Bradley, Susan, Darryle-Anne Jadaa, Joel Brody, Sarah Landry, Susan E. Tallett, William Watson, Barbara Shea, et al. "Brief Psychoeducational Parenting Program: An Evaluation and 1-Year Follow-Up." *Journal of the American Academy of Child and Adolescent Psychiatry* 42, no. 10 (October 2003): 1171–78. doi:10.1097/01.chi.0000081823.25107.75.

Elgar, Frank J., and Patrick J. McGrath. "Self-Administered Psychosocial Treatments for Children and Families." *Journal of Clinical Psychology* 59, no. 3 (2003): 321–39. doi:10.1002/jclp.10132.

Norcross, John C., Linda F. Campbell, John M. Gohol, John W. Santrock, Florin Selagea, and Robert Sommer. *Self-Help That Works: Resources to Improve Emotional Health and Strengthen Relationships*, 162, 165. New York: Oxford University Press, 2013.

Porzig-Drummond, Renata, Richard J. Stevenson, and Carol Stevenson. "The 1-2-3 Magic Parenting Program and Its Effect on Child Problem Behaviors and Dysfunctional Parenting: A Randomized Controlled Trial." *Behaviour Research and Therapy* 58C (May 2014): 52–64. doi: 10.1016/j.brat.2014.05.004.

Salehpour, Yeganeh. "1-2-3 Magic Part I: Its Effectiveness on Parental Function in Child Discipline with Preschool Children." Abstract. *Dissertation Abstracts International*, Section A: Humanities & Social Sciences 57, no 3-A (September 1996): 1009.

Tutty, Steve, Harlan Gephart, and Katie Wurzbacher. "Enhancing Behavioral and Social Skill Functioning in Children Newly Diagnosed with Attention Deficit Hyperactivity Disorder in a Pediatric Setting." *Developmental and Behavioral Pediatrics* 24, no.1 (February 2003): 51–57.

INDEX

A

ADHD (attention-deficit/
hyperactivity disorder), 34
Administrators, 227–236
Age
    elementary grades, 201–204
    middle school, 205–215
    preschool/day care, 193–200
Anger, adult, 17
Apologies, 55
Arguing, 13, 92–94. *See also*
    Little Adult Assumption
Arrival, 140–142
Assemblies, 134–135
Attention-deficit/hyperactivity
    disorder (ADHD), 34
Authoritarian teaching style,
    21–22, 25, 39, 228
Authoritative teaching style, 21,
    23–24, 153–155
Authority, 38–39
Autism, 221–222

B

Badgering, 73–74, 90, 91, 92
Behavior
    discussing with students, 161–167
    ignoring, 51–52
    learning, 165–166 (*See also*
        Training)
    managing, 24–25 (*See also*
        Counting; Stop behavior)
    reinforcement of, 229
    responsibility for, 203
    as separate from person, 79,
        173–174
    teaching, 3–4 (*See also*
        Training)
    types of, 7–10 (*See also* Start
        behavior; Stop behavior)
Behavioral Accounting Form,
    212–215
Behavioral Accounting (or
    Step) System, 212–215
Behavior stoplight, 62, 66, 67

Bullying, 58, 136, 138
Butter up, 76–77, 92

C
Charting, 121–123
Checklist, self-evaluation,
   237–244
Chores, classroom, 145–148
Class meetings, 156–160
Classroom incentives, 132–133,
   209–210
Cleaning up, 146–148
Competition, and classroom
   jobs, 148
Conduct disorder (CD), 96–97
Conferences, with students,
   163–164
Conflicts, 57–59, 84–86
Consequences, natural, 121, 141
Consistency, 129, 130, 186,
   188–189
Cooperator, immediate, 6, 82
Counting, 9, 24, 25, 29
   benefits of, 37–40
   challenges, 33–37, 42–56
   and different misbehaviors, 45–46
   examples, 84–94
   groups, 56, 211
   and opportunity to learn, 55
   preparing students for, 62–68
   in preschool, 196
   procedure, 30–33
   and punishment, 39–40 (*See also*
      Punishment; Time-outs)

at recess, 136–138
and self-esteem, 54
and Start behavior, 89, 124–125
starting over, 43–44
by students, 49–50
and sympathetic listening,
   180–181, 182–185
time between counts, 42–43, 66
tracking, 66–68
and visitors, 52–53
and visual cues, 196
window of opportunity, 43–44, 66

D
Day care, 193–200
Demanding, 21–24
Destinations, 131
Detached teaching style, 21, 23,
   25, 150–152
Disabilities, students with,
   216–223
Discipline, effective
   and getting work done, 149
   steps in, xv–xvi
Discipline, preventive, x, xv
Discipline, serious issues in,
   95–106
Dismissal, 142–143
Disrespect, 138
Docking system, 118–120,
   147–148
Downtime, xiv–xv

E

Elementary grades, 201–204
Embarrassment, 65
Emotion, 16–18, 34, 45. *See
also* No Emotion rule
Emotional disability (ED),
219–220
Expectations, 63
and classroom jobs, 146
and teenagers, 207
Explanations, 13–15, 38, 162, 165

F

Field trips, 133–134
Fighting, 137–138
Fines, 48, 147–148
Forgiveness, 171, 174–175
Frustration, child's, 71–72
Fun, 171, 173, 175

G

Games, 210–211
Greeting students, 140–141, 206
Group incentives, 132–133,
209–210

H

Hallways, 130–132
Health issues, xi
Hearing impairments, 223
Home/school coordination, 40,
186, 188–189

I

Incentives, classroom/group,
132–133, 209–210
Intellectual disability, 220–221
Interrupting, 90–92
Intimidation, 74, 88, 90, 91, 92

J

Jobs, classroom, 145–148

L

Learning, by children, 165–
166
Learning disability (LD),
217–218
Lectures, 120, 174
Lines, 130–132
Listening, sympathetic, 176–
185, 198
Little Adult Assumption,
12–14, 34, 36, 39, 120, 129,
137, 174
Lunchtime, 139
Lying, 103–106

M

Major/Minor System, 98–103
Manipulation. *See* Testing and
manipulation
Martyrdom, 75, 79, 91, 92
Meetings, with students,
163–164

Mental health, xi
  attention-deficit/hyperactivity
    disorder (ADHD), 34
  conduct disorder (CD), 96–97
  oppositional defiant disorder
    (ODD), 97
Middle school, 205–215
Mild intellectual disability
  (MID), 220–221
Motivation, 43
  charting, 121–123
  and serious behavioral
    problems, 96
  for Start behavior, 9, 109
  for Stop behavior, 9
Motivation, extrinsic, 48
Music, and classroom jobs,
  146–147

N
Natural consequences, 121, 141
No Emotion rule, 20, 30, 40,
  120, 131
  and elementary students, 204
  forgetting, 33
  and intervening in fights, 137
  and refusal to go to time-outs,
    46, 47–48
  and students with emotional
    disability, 219
  and testing, 79, 83
No Talking rule, 20, 30, 34–35, 40
  and elementary students, 204
  forgetting, 33

  and intervening in fights, 137
  and refusal to go to time-outs,
    46, 47–48
  and students with emotional
    disability, 219
  and testing, 79, 83

O
Offenses
  first-time, 99
  repeat, 100–103
  serious, 95–106
Office referrals, 228–229
1-2-3 Magic program
  adapting, 130–139
  effectiveness of, 5
  explanation of, 3–6
  implementing, 110, 202
Oppositional defiant disorder
  (ODD), 97

P
Parents, 236
  and administrators, 229, 230–231
  communicating with, 5, 187–189
  orientation to counting, 65
  working with, 186–189
Peer pressure, 210
Permissive teaching style, 21,
  22–23, 25, 228
Persistence, 14
Persuasion, 13. *See also* Little
  Adult Assumption

Phrasing, of requests, 117
Physical contact, 47
  fighting, 137–138
  as testing, 77
Playground, 135–138
Positive reinforcement, 112–115
  and classroom jobs, 148
  during transitions, 143
Pouting, 59
Power, 17
Power struggles, 204, 207
Praise, 113–115, 141, 171,
  172–173, 175, 196–197, 235
Preschool, 193–200
Principals, 227–236
Problem-solving, 156
Punishment. *See also* Time-out
  alternatives; Time-outs
  connection with behavior, 41
  and counting, 39–40
  Major/Minor System, 98–103
  and peer conflict, 59
  for serious offenses, 98–103

Q

Questions, and discussing
  behavior issues, 164–165
Quick Exit Routine, 50–51

R

Reason, 13, 34. *See also* Little
  Adult Assumption
Recess, 135–138

Record keeping, 212–215
Rehearsal, 141
Reinforcement
  and serious behavioral
    problems, 96
  positive, 112–115
Reinforcers, natural *vs.*
  artificial, 122–123
Relationships, strengthening,
  24–25, 100, 171–189, 236
  sympathetic listening, 176–185
  with teenagers, 206–207
  working with parents, 186–189
Repetition, 14, 165
Requests
  simple, 115–117, 125–126
  spontaneous, 117, 118
Revenge, 78–79
Routines, 111
  arrival, 140–142
  dismissal, 142–143
  rehearsing, 127, 141
Rules, 65, 207–210
Running away, 74, 77

S

Schoolwork, and discipline, xv,
  149–155
Self-esteem, 54, 79, 92, 171,
  177–178
Slipping, 248–249
Social skills, 159–160
Special needs students, 216–223
Spontaneity, 117, 118

Start behavior, 7, 8, 10, 235
    for completing classroom jobs,
       145–148
    and counting, 89, 124–125
    getting schoolwork done,
       149–155
    motivation for, 9, 109
    for moving between activities,
       140–144
    and need for training, 112 (See
       also Training)
    tactics for, 8, 111–127
    and testing and manipulation,
       111
Stop behavior, 7, 10, 235
    motivation for, 9
    and serious offenses, 95–106
    tactics for, 8 (See also
       Counting)
Stoplight, behavior, 62, 66, 67
Sympathetic listening, 100,
    176–185, 198

T
Talking, 13–15, 16–18, 34, 38,
    45. See also No Talking rule
Talk-Persuade-Argue-Yell-
    Hit syndrome, 13, 15, 16,
    38, 129. See also Little Adult
    Assumption
Tantrums
    adult, 13, 120
    child, 60–61, 74, 199–200. See
       also Intimidation

Teachers
    authority of, 38–39
    hiring, 232–234
    personal lives, 172–173
    self-evaluation checklist,
       237–244
Teaching
    effective, xv, 149, 155, 234
    style, 20–25, 150–152
Teaching, vs. parenting, xiv–xv
Teasing, 88–89
Teenagers, 205–215
Temper. See Intimidation
Testing and manipulation, xiv,
    72–83, 88
    managing, 80–81, 82–83,
       90–93, 105
    mechanics of, 77–78
    purposes of, 78–79
    and Start behavior tactics, 111
    tactics, 73–77
    tactic switching, 82
    whining, 81
Threats, 74–75, 77, 88
Time, and sympathetic
    listening, 181–182
Time-out alternatives (TOAs),
    31, 40–41, 53
Time-outs, 31
    area, 44–45
    effectiveness of, 45
    in elementary school, 203
    for entire class, 56
    on field trips, 134
    leaving, 53–54

in preschool, 195, 197, 198

at recess, 138

refusal to go to, 46–49

Timers, 118, 147

Token economy system

docking system, 118–120, 147–148

fines, 48

Training, 14, 112, 141, 142, 146

Transitions, 143–144

V

Visitors, and counting, 52–53

Visual cues, 196

Visual impairments, 223

Voice, 116, 196

W

Warmth, 21–24

Warnings, 31, 34. *See also*
  Counting

Whining, 81

Window of opportunity,
  43–44, 66

Y

Yelling, 138

ABOUT THE AUTHORS

DR. THOMAS W. PHELAN is an internationally renowned expert, author, and lecturer on child discipline and attention deficit disorder. A registered PhD clinical psychologist, he appears frequently on radio and TV. Dr. Phelan practices and works in the western suburbs of Chicago.

SARAH JANE SCHONOUR is a National Board Certified Teacher with more than twenty-five years of experience in the field of education. She received her undergraduate degree from the College of William and Mary and her master's degree from George Washington University. Mrs. Schonour has served as adjunct faculty for two universities in the Washington, DC area.

IF YOU LOVED *1-2-3 MAGIC* IN THE CLASSROOM...

check out these other products from Thomas W. Phelan, PhD

1-2-3 Magic
Effective Discipline for Children 2–12

1-2-3 Magic DVD
Managing Difficult Behavior in Children 2–12

More *1-2-3 Magic* DVD
Encouraging Good Behavior, Independence, and Self-Esteem

1-2-3 Magic Workbook
A user-friendly, illustrated companion to the *1 2-3 Magic* book that includes case studies, self-evaluation questions, and exercises

1-2-3 Magic for Teachers DVD
Effective Classroom Discipline Pre-K through Grade 8

1-2-3 Magic for Kids
Helping Your Children Understand the New Rules

1-2-3 Magic for Christian Parents
Effective Discipline for Children 2–12

1-2-3 Magic Starter Kit
Accessories to help you get started with the 1-2-3 Magic program

Tantrums! Book and DVD
Managing Meltdowns in Public and Private

1-2-3 Magic Teen
Communicate, Connect, and Guide Your Teen to Adulthood

Did You Know? The *1-2-3 Magic* parenting book and DVDs are also available in Spanish!

Visit www.123magic.com